Ensuring Failure

*Financial System Stability and
Deposit Insurance in Canada*

*J.L. Carr
G.F. Mathewson
N.C. Quigley*

Observation 36
C.D. Howe Institute

P9-BJA-305

C.D. Howe Institute publications are available from:
Renouf Publishing Company Limited, 1294 Algoma Road,
Ottawa, Ontario K1B 3W8; phone (613) 741-4333; fax (613) 741-5439

and from Renouf's stores at:
71½ Sparks Street, Ottawa (613) 238-8985
211 Yonge Street, Toronto (416) 363-3171

For trade book orders, please contact:
McGraw-Hill Ryerson Limited, 300 Water Street,
Whitby, Ontario L1N 9B6; phone (416) 430-5050

Institute publications are also available in microform from:
Micromedia Limited, 165 Hôtel de Ville, Place du Portage, Phase II,
Hull, Quebec J8X 3X2

This book is printed on recycled, acid-free paper.

Canadian Cataloguing in Publication Data

Carr, Jack L., 1944–
    Ensuring failure : financial system stability and
deposit insurance in Canada

(Observation, ISSN 0826-9947 ; 36)
Includes bibliographical references.
ISBN 0-88806-339-3

1. Deposit insurance – Canada. 2. Canada Deposit
Insurance Corporation. I. Mathewson, G. Frank, 1942–   .
II. Quigley, Neil C. (Neil Clayton), 1957–   .
III. C.D. Howe Institute. IV. Title. V. Series:
Observation (C.D. Howe Institute) ; 360.

HG1662.C3C37 1994   368.8'54'00971   C94-930789-0

© C.D. Howe Institute, Toronto.
Quotation with appropriate credit is permissible.

Cover design by Leroux Design Inc.
Printed in Canada by Hignell Printing Limited
Winnipeg, Manitoba, February 1994.

AUGUSTANA LIBRARY
UNIVERSITY OF ALBERTA

Contents

Foreword v

The Study in Brief vii

Acknowledgments xiii

Chapter 1: Efficiency and Political
  Explanations for Deposit Insurance 1
The Economic Efficiency
  Justification for Deposit Insurance 4
The Political Origins of Deposit Insurance 14

Chapter 2: The Banking System before 1967:
  Stability without Deposit Insurance 16
Entry Requirements 17
Bank Failures 21
Bank Mergers 27
The Emergence of Government Inspection 36
Attitudes toward Deposit Insurance 39
What Created Stability from 1924 to 1966? .41

Chapter 3: The Effect of Deposit Insurance
  on the Banking System 43
The Dual Banking System in Canada 43
The Introduction of Deposit Insurance 46
Deposit Insurance and Regional Development 51
Empirical Evidence 54
Conclusion 63
Appendix 65

Chapter 4: Regulation and
  Depositor Compensation 67
CDIC Governance 70
Fine Tuning and Extending the Regulatory System 76
Amalgamation of the CDIC and the OSFI 78
Market Discipline: Coinsurance and Risk Premiums 83
Provincial Jurisdiction and Harmonization of Regulations 89
Conclusion 91

Chapter 5: Conclusions and Recommendations 92
The Rationale for Reform 92
Compensation of Depositors 95
Constitution and Governance of the CDIC 96
The Relationship between the OSFI and the CDIC 98
Effects of Our Recommendations 98

References 101

Tables

1   Failures of Members of the Canada
    Deposit Insurance Corporation, 1967–92 2

2   Entry into and Exit from the
    Canadian Banking System, 1870–1966 19

3   Failures of Canadian Chartered Banks, 1890–1966 20

4   Canadian Chartered Banks
    Absorbed or Merged, 1890–1966 28–29

5   Mergers of Canadian Banks: Share Market Evidence 31

6   Entry of New Provincial (Ontario) and Federal Trust
    and Mortgage Loan Companies, 1949–66 and 1968–85 57

7   Debt-to-Equity Ratios for Chartered Banks and Trust
    and Mortgage Loan Companies, 1949–67 and 1968–85 58

8   Insured Deposits in Trust and Mortgage Loan
    Companies in which the CDIC Intervened 62

9   Minimum Equity Requirements for
    Canadian Financial Institutions 64

10 The Effect of Deposit Insurance on the
    Herfindahl Index of Concentration of Assets 65

11 Estimation of the Debt-to-Equity Equation for
    Chartered Banks and Trust and Mortgage Loan
    Companies, 1949–67 and 1968–85 66

Members of the C.D. Howe Institute 107

Foreword

Watching the unfolding of the US savings and loan debacle — an episode whose ultimate economic impact and cost to the taxpayer has yet to be calculated — Canadians could be forgiven for congratulating themselves on the relative stability and soundness of their own banking and regulatory systems. But the substantial losses recently reported by the Canada Deposit Insurance Corporation serve as a reminder that business and regulatory shortfalls in the deposit-taking industry threaten substantial costs to the public treasury — and to the broader economy — in Canada as well.

The increasing size, complexity, and integration of the financial industry in Canada and around the world mean that containing these risks will be a key, if not always high-profile, public policy issue in Canada in the years ahead. The nature and extent of publicly mandated deposit insurance is a central aspect of this task.

For this reason, the C.D. Howe Institute is pleased to publish this study of deposit insurance in Canada by Professors Jack Carr, Frank Mathewson, and Neil Quigley. Their analysis of the economics of deposit insurance, their thorough survey of the historical circumstances that have affected Canada's experience, and their policy recommendations are important reading for industry specialists, policymakers, and all those whose lives and businesses are touched by Canada's depository institutions.

The C.D. Howe Institute's aim is to raise the level of public debate on issues of national interest by presenting diverse points of view — whether or not it agrees with them — in publications that are well researched and well grounded. The Institute believes that, in so doing, it can help Canadians make informed decisions about difficult policy issues.

This study was edited by Lenore d'Anjou, Riça Night, and Barry A. Norris, and desktop published by Brenda Palmer. The analysis and opinions presented in the study are the responsibility of the authors and do not necessarily reflect the views of the Institute's members or Board of Directors.

Thomas E. Kierans
President and
Chief Executive Officer

The Study in Brief

The Canada Deposit Insurance Corporation (CDIC) is a Crown corporation created by an act of Parliament in 1967. Its statutory objects are to

- insure certain deposits in member institutions up to a limit currently set at $60,000 for each account;
- promote standards of sound business and financial practices for member institutions;
- promote the stability and competitiveness of the financial system in Canada; and
- pursue these objects "in such manner as will minimize the exposure of the Corporation to loss."

Members of the CDIC pay premiums within a range established by statute and determined by the corporation's Board so as to provide sufficient income to meet payments to depositors, interest charges, and operational expenditures. Taxpayers have no explicit liability for losses resulting from the operation of the CDIC.

Most studies of deposit insurance in Canada and elsewhere maintain that it has been introduced to enhance economic efficiency. They claim that it does this by preventing bank runs, promoting competition, extending to all banks and institutions the implicit guarantee that governments are said to give to very large banks, and redressing the failure of private markets to provide insurance for depositors. In contrast to this efficiency hypothesis, it can be argued that, at least in Canada, the primary objective of deposit insurance is to impose a specific tax on the large chartered banks and on a small number of conservatively managed trust companies. Deposit insurance is used to provide a subsidy to politically important high-risk and regionally concentrated deposit-taking institutions: it enhances the viability of such institutions and encourages entry to the industry. But, by removing the threat of loss from deposit accounts of $60,000 or less, deposit insurance has reduced market discipline on management and increased the returns to imprudence and fraud. Providing depositors with 100 percent insurance against loss has ensured higher rates of failure among banks, trust, and mortgage loan companies, and reduced the stability of the financial system.

Chapter 2 analyzes the operation of the Canadian banking system in the period before 1967. New evidence from the archives of the Canadian Bankers' Association and the Department of Finance is used to test and reject the assertion that stability in this period rested on an implicit guarantee of deposits. The evidence suggests that, after 1923, bank failures in which depositors' funds might have been lost were avoided through

- the absence of 100 percent deposit insurance;
- the safeguards provided by independent audits conducted on behalf of both the government and the shareholders; and
- government sanction of a market-driven merger movement.

A 100 percent guarantee of deposits would, in fact, have removed the market mechanism that facilitated a stable banking system.

As Chapter 3 shows, the CDIC was established in a period of relative financial stability — that is, there was no general crisis among deposit-taking institutions and no evidence of system-wide withdrawals of funds. The problem addressed by deposit insurance was depositor awareness of the high risk associated with the provincially chartered trust and mortgage loan companies. Legal precedent and federal-provincial relations militated against federal jurisdiction being directly extended over these institutions. The enacted scheme offered the politically expedient compromise: it induced provincial regulators to make membership of the scheme compulsory for the institutions they supervised.

The evidence clearly shows that deposit insurance increased both insolvencies and the instability of the Canadian financial system. Insolvencies have been confined to two types of institutions: new entrants that strategically exploited the subsidy provided by deposit insurance; and institutions with very high proportions of their deposits insured and that were subject to little depositor monitoring. In both cases, the underlying causes of the problem are likely the loss of market discipline and the incentive for financial entrepreneurs to dissipate the money of shareholders and CDIC members in undiversified and high-risk loan portfolios, which are associated with deposit insurance.

Supporters of Canada's current deposit insurance scheme hold that it is instrumental in fostering competition with the chartered banks. But the evidence clearly proves that deposit insurance has failed either to compensate for regulatory impediments to competition or to subsidize the growth of competitive firms. The incentive for imprudence provided by deposit insurance has outweighed any of the claimed beneficial effects and has reduced — rather than increased — the number of viable and independent competitors for the large chartered banks.

In the face of the excessive levels of risk taking promoted by deposit insurance, regulators have proved unable to ensure diligent management and have frequently proved unable to make timely and accurate assessments of the solvency of institutions. This regulatory failure results primarily from the current structure of deposit insurance and regulation, not from the actions of individual officials. The governance structure of the CDIC and the organization of the Office of the Superintendent of Financial Institutions (OSFI) do not provide appropriate incentives for and accountability by the officials who manage the system. In particular,

- the CDIC has multiple, potentially contradictory, objectives;
- the CDIC Board and staff are accountable to the government rather than to the institutions that fund the scheme; and
- the public regulatory authority for deposit-taking institutions, the OSFI, is not liable for the quality and accuracy of the assessments of firm solvency that it provides to the CDIC.

The approaches to reform advocated by the CDIC and the OSFI involve increasing control over the management of deposit-taking institutions, instituting new and more complex evaluation criteria to guide regulatory activities, and hiring more regulators. Canada's current system of deposit insurance has relied too much on regulators' ability to prevent failures of financial institutions and to minimize the loss of capital in insolvent institutions. Regulators' increasing tendency to manage deposit-taking institutions is inappropriate. They lack both the practical knowledge and the pecuniary incentives for effective management of the deposit insurance system. Their efforts to assist weak institutions have generally been unsuccessful in restoring financial health and have substantially increased losses of uninsured creditors and CDIC members.

Reforms that subject depository institutions and the regulators to increased market discipline hold the greatest potential for ameliorating and removing the problems currently associated with deposit insurance. The most effective reform strategy would be the introduction of coinsurance at a level that would establish the type of market discipline that prevailed in Canada before 1967. This would require a significant reduction in the coverage of deposit insurance; a reasonable maximum limit of such coverage would be 80 percent. The following recommendations therefore seem in order:

- The coverage provided by the CDIC should be reduced to 80 percent of the first $60,000 of a deposit.
- When insolvent institutions are sold as going concerns, coinsurance should be enforced by the apportioning of losses to insured and uninsured deposit accounts.

Coinsurance does not require that all depositors be able to determine precisely the financial position of a deposit-taking institution. It gives depositors an incentive to use the information that they do have when placing a deposit, and it encourages individual institutions, as well as regulators, to increase the flow of credible information to depositors.

. The CDIC must accept the principle of management by the institutions with wealth at stake. Specifically:

- The CDIC should be reconstituted with the member institutions as shareholders.
- The CDIC should be managed by a Board elected from its shareholders, with appropriate allowance for representation of different types of institutions.
- The CDIC's actions should be made publicly accountable through a legislative directive on the compensation of depositors and through the appointment of one member of the Board.

Compulsory membership of the CDIC is unjustifiable. Making membership voluntary would highlight the primacy of the political motivation for Canada's deposit insurance scheme and spur the quest for more efficient means of providing low-risk savings instruments for unsophisticated depositors. Voluntary membership would also promote the competitiveness and stability of the financial system. Thus, when the coinsurance ratio of 80 percent is reached after two years, membership of the CDIC should become voluntary.

Amalgamating the OSFI and the CDIC would not provide sufficient incentive for them to make timely and accurate assessments of the solvency of financial institutions; nor would it increase their accountability for their diligence in obtaining and providing information. Such an amalgamation might make these problems worse. To improve accountability and promote incentives for accurate assessments of solvency, the inspection and audit services now provided by the OSFI should be privatized. The OSFI should purchase these services from the most effective supplier when they are required to supplement market information and statutory returns.

Acknowledgments

This study began after we had completed a paper on the introduction of deposit insurance in Canada. David Laidler encouraged us to consider expanding the work through more detailed historical research and more explicit investigation of the policy implications of our views. He has been instrumental in guiding the results through to the publication of this monograph. Ron Shearer's constructive skepticism and encouragement have greatly enhanced the quality of our arguments. Shawn Cooper, Ian Drummond, John Evans, Ramsay Holmes, Ig Horstmann, Lawrie Masterman, Peter Maurice, Russell Morrison, Anne Riley, Michael Shadbolt, and Helen Sinclair have discussed the issues with us and have saved us from many errors of fact and interpretation. Naturally, we absolve all of these people of any responsibility for both the remaining errors and the views that we have expressed.

We thank the staff of the Canadian Bankers' Association and the Canada Deposit Insurance Corporation for their assistance with the compilation of the data, and Yvonne Adams for typing the tables. Financial support from the University of Western Ontario and the Institute for Policy Analysis at the University of Toronto is gratefully acknowledged.

Jack Carr,
Frank Mathewson,
Neil Quigley

Chapter 1

Efficiency and Political Explanations for Deposit Insurance

Federal deposit insurance in Canada is provided by the Canada Deposit Insurance Corporation (CDIC), created by an act of Parliament in 1967 to guarantee certain types of deposits of member institutions up to a limit currently set at $60,000 for each account.[1] While the CDIC is a publicly mandated and managed Crown corporation, it is privately funded. There is no statutory commitment of public funds for capital or operating subsidies. All administrative costs, interest charges on funds borrowed by the CDIC from the consolidated revenue fund, and net payments to depositors in insolvent institutions are funded from CDIC member contributions.

For 15 years, net CDIC payments to depositors were small. Since 1983, however, the number of failures and the magnitude of the resulting losses suffered by member institutions have increased support for the view that the current framework for deposit insurance should be substantially reformed (see Table 1). The cost of operating the CDIC from 1967 to 1992, as estimated on April 1, 1993, was $3.59 billion. Premiums assessed from member institutions totaled $2.09 billion, leaving a deficit as at year end 1992 of $1.50 bil-

---

1 All federally incorporated banks and trust and mortgage loan companies are compelled to be members of the CDIC. The trust and loan companies incorporated by all provinces except Quebec are also members. Quebec has a separate Deposit Insurance Board, which was established in parallel with the CDIC in 1967.

Table 1: *Failures of Members of the Canada Deposit Insurance Corporation, 1967–92*

Year	Institution	Payments/ Exposure	Losses
		($ millions, estimated)	
1970	Commonwealth Trust Company	5	0
1972	Security Trust Company Limited	9	0
1980	Astra Trust Company	21	3
1982	District Trust Company	231	15
1983	Amic Mortgage Investment Corporation	28	15
1983	Crown Trust Company	930	5
1983	Fidelity Trust Company	791	359
1983	Greymac Mortgage Corporation	174	106
1983	Greymac Trust Company	240	150
1983	Seaway Mortgage Corporation	120	4
1983	Seaway Trust Company	300	73
1984	Northguard Mortgage Corporation	28	8
1985	Continental Trust Company	113	0
1985	Pioneer Trust Company	201	27
1985	Western Capital Trust Company	77	3
1985	Canadian Commercial Bank	352	243
1985	CCB Mortgage Investment Corporation	36	13
1985	London Loan Limited	24	5
1985	Northland Bank	318	161
1986	Bank of British Columbia	200	200
1986	Columbia Trust Company	99	0
1987	North West Trust Company	275	275
1987	Principal Savings & Trust Company	116	0
1988	Financial Trust Company	74	n.a.
1991	Bank of Credit & Commerce Canada	22	n.a.
1991	Standard Trust Company	1,326	n.a.
1991	Saskatchewan Trust Company	58	13
1992	First City Trust Company	500	n.a.
1992	Shoppers Trust Company	500	n.a.
1992	Central Guaranty Trust Company	4,400	n.a.

Sources: Canada Deposit Insurance Corporation, *Annual Report 1991*; and authors' calculations.

lion (Canada Deposit Insurance Corporation, Corporate Communications, August 31, 1993).

The House of Commons Standing Committee on Finance (Canada 1992a) suggested that the problems associated with deposit insurance in Canada are so serious that a re-examination should be undertaken of some of the basic principles on which such a scheme is based. What does deposit insurance try to do? Who, and what, does it try to protect? What are the unintended consequences of the current system? In this study, we answer some of these questions, using an economic analysis of the history, introduction, and current operation of deposit insurance in Canada.

Most studies of deposit insurance in Canada and elsewhere maintain that it has been introduced to enhance economic efficiency.[2] It purports to do this by preventing bank runs, promoting competition, extending to all banks and institutions the implicit guarantee that governments are said to give to very large banks, and redressing the failure of private markets to provide insurance for depositors. In contrast to this efficiency hypothesis, we argue that, at least in Canada, the primary objective of deposit insurance is political. The deposit insurance scheme managed by the CDIC imposes a specific tax on the large chartered banks and on a small number of conservatively managed trust companies. The tax is used to provide a subsidy to politically important high-risk and regionally concentrated deposit-taking institutions. This transfer of wealth has helped both to increase entry to the industry and to sustain the viability of provincial jurisdiction over depository institutions. While Canada's deposit insurance scheme serves these political imperatives, it has

---

2 Economic efficiency is achieved when the economy operates in a manner that ensures that no one could be made better off without making someone else worse off. Economic efficiency assumes that gainers compensate losers, so that a move toward efficiency requires an increase in the aggregate value of the net worth of an economy. Assertions that deposit insurance increases economic efficiency mean that it meets two objectives: (1) *cost minimization* — the cost of providing a given amount of financial intermediation is lower with deposit insurance than it is without it; and (2) *output enhancement* — more services are provided with deposit insurance than would be available without it.

promoted institutions and policies that have substantially impaired the stability and efficiency of the financial system.

The Economic Efficiency Justification for Deposit Insurance

Runs by Depositors and Financial System Stability

Many economists believe that deposit insurance promotes economic efficiency. Macroeconomic shocks to the financial system and contagious runs by imperfectly informed depositors may cause the supply of money (Friedman and Schwartz 1963) or credit (Bernanke 1983) to contract. When one institution becomes insolvent and depositors believe that all firms may be unable to honor their deposit contracts, a "run" may occur — that is, depositors attempt to withdraw their funds from a financial institution before similar action by other depositors forces it to suspend payment. Friedman and Schwartz (1963, 434) argued that, in the United States, deposit insurance was

> the most important structural change in the banking system to result from the 1933 panic, and, indeed, in [their] view the structural change most conducive to monetary stability since state bank note issues were taxed out of existence immediately after the Civil War.

Subsequent research has developed formal models in which illiquid, but otherwise solvent, deposit-taking institutions with demand liabilities may be subject to runs by depositors unless deposit insurance is provided.[3]

When depositors run on a single solvent institution, its managers may reassure depositors by rediscounting assets with other private sector institutions or the central bank to obtain liquidity; they

---

3 For example, Diamond and Dybvig 1983; Jacklin and Bhattacharya 1988; and Postelwaite and Vives 1987.

may also release credible financial information. The case for eliminating runs by imperfectly informed depositors is therefore strongest when these runs are so widespread that they threaten the viability of the whole system and when central banking facilities are either absent or unable to deal with the magnitude of the problem. The failure of the banking system in the United States during the Great Depression is often cited as an example of the implications of imperfect information, but this assertion is open to dispute. The view that runs by US depositors represented the rational response to the widespread insolvency of state and small national banks appears to us to be a credible alternative.

In Canada, the claimed causal link between macroeconomic shocks, contagious runs, and failures of deposit-taking institutions, on the one hand, and deposit insurance, on the other, appears to be unsubstantiated. No Canadian banks failed during the Great Depression, and there have been no system-wide withdrawals of funds by depositors in the past 100 years. The Bank of Canada has, in the past, made some substantial liquidity loans to institutions experiencing losses of deposits.[4] We know of no documented instance in which a well-managed Canadian institution has been forced into insolvency as a result of a run by depositors.[5] We show in Chapter 3 that attempts (such as by Cameron [1992, 339]) to explain the introduction of the CDIC in 1967 by citing the threat of contagion effects from the failure of a trust company are implausible and are not supported by empirical evidence.

---

4 See the discussion of the failure of the CCB and the Northland Bank in Chapter 3. Central bank loans to an insolvent institution whose financial position is deteriorating are problematical because they may serve to increase the losses experienced by unsecured creditors when the institution is finally closed.

5 The Continental Bank of Canada (purchased by Lloyds Bank Canada in October 1986) and the Mercantile Bank of Canada (purchased by the National Bank of Canada in February 1986) are sometimes portrayed as victims of runs by imperfectly informed depositors in the aftermath of the failure of the Canadian Commercial Bank (CCB) and the Northland Bank. As the discussion in Chapter 3 reveals, there is no evidence that the actions of depositors should be interpreted as anything other than an effective mechanism for the identification of weak banks whose assets were more valuable when merged with a stronger institution.

Our approach does not deny the potential importance of macroeconomic shocks or regulatory changes in influencing the precise timing of bank failures. We believe, however, that focusing on macroeconomic shocks offers little insight into the fundamental causes of the introduction of deposit insurance and the failure of insured banks. Studies with such a focus cannot explain why a number of large Canadian banks have remained solvent during every macroeconomic shock, including the Great Depression, since the first half of the nineteenth century; nor can they explain why these large banks appear to have been relatively immune to the moral hazard resulting from the introduction of deposit insurance.[6]

While the benefits of removing all motivation for depositors to run on financial institutions are uncertain, the costs associated with the introduction of 100 percent deposit insurance are clear-cut. In the absence of deposit insurance, rational runs by depositors will provide the discipline essential to the smooth functioning and stability of the banking system. The threat of withdrawal by depositors will force institutions sustaining losses to implement credible policies designed to restore solvency. If the management and shareholders do not do this, depositors may withdraw funds from the institution in an attempt to close it before it suffers losses in excess of the buffer provided by shareholder equity. In such cases, the actions of depositors will also serve as a check on the regulators and provide incentives for effective regulatory action on weak deposit-taking institutions.

Competition

A persistent theme of the Canadian literature has maintained that deposit insurance was introduced to increase the competitiveness of the financial system (Binhammer and Boulakia 1968, 39; Schwartz 1993, 8; Shearer, Chant, and Bond 1984, 362–3). The president of the Trust Companies Association recently argued that the subsidy pro-

---

6 Moral hazard (hidden action) is associated with deposit insurance because such insurance provides the managers of insured firms with an incentive to assume greater risk than they would otherwise take.

vided by the CDIC to most members of the association is justified because

> [t]he cost to Canada of all the failures of financial institutions in our history has been but a drop in the bucket in comparison to the billions upon billions we have spent bailing out inefficient industrial firms and subsidizing unworkable regional development schemes, not to mention the billions spent each year subsidizing Canadian agriculture. Indeed, I contend that the increased efficiency brought about by the more dynamic financial institutions has paid for any failures many times over. (Evans 1992, 6.)

It seems unlikely that competition was more than a secondary motivation for the introduction of deposit insurance — otherwise the government would have created a more direct and efficient means of reducing barriers to entry and increasing competition between the banks and other financial institutions. In addition, the idea seems questionable that the CDIC has provided a vehicle for enhanced efficiency resulting from increased competition — that is, that the cost of the subsidy received by many members of the Trust Companies Association is justified. It has encouraged new entrants, but entry alone is neither necessary nor sufficient for competitive efficiency.[7] The major positive innovations and competitive pressures introduced to retail banking in the past decade appear to have been provided by the established trust companies whose growth and viability did not require deposit insurance. In contrast to institutions that concentrate on the domestic Canadian market, the large Canadian banks have extensive operations in international wholesale markets where the banks' attractiveness to depositors does not rest on the existence of the CDIC.[8] So long as the banks are competitive

---

7 An efficient system requires that entry be possible — that there be a contestable market — but it does not require that entry actually occur. Subsidized entry does not necessarily promote efficiency.

8 The Economic Council of Canada (1976) argued that the CDIC provided benefits for the international business of Canadian banks, since it meant that foreign depositors knew that Canadian banks would not fail because of runs by imperfectly...

in these large and relatively unregulated markets and cannot discriminate against customers in Canada, there is no clear rationale for government attempts to increase the number of deposit-taking firms. Small, regionally concentrated institutions will be justified if they occupy a market niche ignored by the banks or possess some technology that provides them with a competitive advantage in the local market. In either of these cases, they would be viable without a subsidy.

Entry subsidies of the type provided by the CDIC are not wealth neutral — that is, they will have implications for the aggregate wealth of the economy. Subsidies reduce the aggregate wealth of Canadians. This is because subsidies promote an allocation of resources among different competing uses that is inferior to the allocation produced by market forces. In addition, the expenditure of resources on rent seeking (such as lobbying for subsidies) reduces wealth because it is socially unproductive. Horstmann and Markusen (1986) show that, in industries where increasing returns to scale favor the emergence of a small number of large firms but where entry is open,[9] efficiency will not be improved by subsidies that favor new entrants. Entry will be driven by the desire to obtain subsidies, rather than by the ability to compete in the market. The results of Horstmann and Markusen would be even more clear-cut in an industry where the subsidy is provided by a specific tax on internationally competitive incumbent firms, as is the case with deposit insurance in Canada. The subsidy to entrants would cause their output to expand, but would also cause aggregated average costs to rise and the output

---

Note 8 - cont'd.

   ...informed depositors. This benefit, if it exists at all, is outweighed by the costs to the large chartered banks of the subsidy that their CDIC premiums provide to high-risk domestic institutions. At current premium levels, the effect of CDIC membership on the international competitiveness of the large Canadian chartered banks appears to us to be negative rather than positive.

9 Entry was historically less open before 1980 than it has been since the early 1980s, but new entry was always possible. Current entry policies are sufficiently open to provide for contestable markets for banks and trust companies (Nathan and Neave 1989).

of incumbents to fall; the net effect on economic welfare as a whole would be negative.

The applicability of these arguments to deposit insurance in Canada is clear. It seems plausible that deposit insurance has increased total financial intermediation in the Canadian economy, but inefficient new entrants — undisciplined by depositors — have dissipated hundreds of millions of dollars on impecunious borrowers involved in high-risk activities.

Since the net losses associated with this activity have been borne by the CDIC, it has raised the costs and thus reduced the competitiveness and output of the remaining solvent firms. We estimate that CDIC premiums of one-tenth of 1 percent amounted to 7 percent of the total pre-tax income of banks operating in Canada in 1992.[10] With an increase in the premium rates to one-eighth of 1 percent of insured deposits in 1993, and the acquisition of the assets of Royal Trust and Central Guaranty Trust by banks, we estimate that CDIC premiums may have represented as much as 10 percent of the pre-tax income of the banks in 1993. By 1994, when premiums are scheduled to increase to one-sixth of 1 percent, the charge on the banks could be as high as 12 percent of pre-tax income. Of course, if the data were available to calculate these figures as a proportion of the profits earned on the banks' Canadian business, the tax resulting from the operation of the CDIC would appear to be even more severe.

The moral hazard related to deposit insurance has also severely limited the emergence of firms that are able to compete directly with the big six chartered banks. For many institutions, the incentive for excessive risk taking is greater than the impact of the direct subsidy received. As a result, they have either failed or been purchased by banks after losses impaired their capital.[11] Even among the larger

---

10 Our calculations assume that, in 1992, banks paid 70 percent of CDIC premium income, estimated at $300 million.

11 Of the five largest trust companies operating in 1990 (Zelmer 1991), only Canada Trust and National Trust have survived the recent recession as independent firms. Central Guaranty Trust and Royal Trust have failed; Montreal Trust sustained major losses and has been purchased by the Bank of Nova Scotia.

trust companies, deposit insurance has actually had the effect of reducing the number of firms competing in the market. Competition is likely to be further inhibited if this increased risk taking results in increased regulation of the business of financial institutions.

Market Failure: Imperfect Information and Moral Hazard

Imperfectly informed depositors are often used to justify another argument: since most small, unsophisticated depositors are either unable to assess the soundness of different financial intermediaries or can do so only at prohibitive cost, deposit insurance may be regarded as a social program provided for their protection. The monitoring of financial intermediaries by individuals with small amounts of wealth to invest is undoubtedly costly, but there is no reason to believe that monitoring is required by such individuals for markets to function efficiently. Large depositors have an incentive to monitor, and this provides discipline for the institution as well as information to other depositors.[12] In the absence of deposit insurance, banks themselves have incentives to generate credible and accessible information on their solvency as a means of competing for depositors. Private rating agencies or a public auditor may also provide assessments of the strength of intermediaries. Government audit and dissemination of data on the operations of financial intermediaries need not imply responsibility for losses sustained by depositors.

None of the foregoing arguments means that we view monitoring by depositors as a perfect mechanism for the discipline of bank managers; the potential for fraud always exists, and can result in losses to depositors. We simply believe that it is incorrect to assume that depositors lack useful information about bank quality. Consequently,

---

12 As Stigler (1974) pointed out, free riding does not mean that market mechanisms will be inoperative. So long as some depositors do undertake monitoring, then the ability of any institution to retain or attract deposits will be influenced by the policies of its management.

it is inefficient to remove all incentives for them to use the information that they do have. Even though depositors may have imperfect information about the actions of bank management, their having wealth at stake means that they will be more effective than regulators in using the information that is available to identify weak management and promote a market resolution of the resulting problems.

Schwartz (1993) treats Canada's deposit insurance scheme as a true scheme of insurance — that is, an attempt to provide a socially optimal reduction in aggregate risk bearing by pooling individual exposures.[13] Mutual deposit insurance schemes have, however, been established only when governments have imposed them by legislation. This suggests that government action may have been prompted by market failure. Such failure is usually said to occur because moral hazard (hidden action) and adverse selection (hidden information) are associated with deposit insurance: firms with high-risk portfolios are most likely to seek insurance and, after obtaining it, may take actions that will increase even further the likelihood of the insurance being required. But moral hazard is associated with all insurance contracts — since high-risk activities may be undertaken once insurance is obtained — and it is not clear that the insurance of deposits is any different. Moreover, government involvement in the provision of insurance does not solve the moral hazard problem, so there is no obvious efficiency gain from the imposition of public deposit insurance schemes.

Our view is that the absence of private deposit insurance indicates a lack of demand for it as an insurance product. Individual depositors get a diversified asset base from any well-managed institution and can insure against management failure at trivial cost by diversifying their deposits among institutions. Further diversification has been made possible by the technological advances that have dramatically increased the availability of mutual funds. The value of funds invested in Canadian mutual funds reached $100 billion

---

13 This line of argument justifies the compulsory nature of Canada's deposit insurance scheme by the need to get a large pool of risks and avoid adverse selection (the withdrawal of the low-risk firms from the scheme).

during 1993, indicating that as much as one-sixth of personal "deposits" may now be held in this form. If provincial regulations that currently prohibit the "sweeping" of balances from bank deposit accounts into low-risk instruments — such as treasury bill mutual funds — are removed, the necessity of insuring deposit accounts will be open to serious question.[14] If we are correct in believing that the primary rationale for the existence of deposit insurance is the provision of subsidies, it is no surprise that the private sector does not provide it.

Too Big to Fail

The final public interest rationale for deposit insurance is the hypothesis labeled "too big to fail." Some institutions are considered to be so large that their failure would paralyze the payments system of the economy; thus, government inevitably would bail them out should they become insolvent. The problem is that managers who believe that their institutions are in this category will not join a deposit insurance scheme voluntarily, but must be forced to join so that they pay premiums for the implicit coverage that they in fact obtain from government.

Kaufman (1989) argues that there is no economic rationale for the too-big-to-fail hypothesis. His arguments are directly applicable to Canada. The failure of any single, large institution has minimal implications for the economy because its business will be attractive to one of its domestic or international competitors, at a price determined by the value of the equity. Disruption to the payments system would be minimal so long as any losses are apportioned among the depositors and the business of the institution continues under new management.

The too-big-to-fail hypothesis may, however, be stronger when it is linked to political motivations. If the depositors of a large bank

---

14 These developments also seem to us to make redundant the suggestion that regulations provide for insured and uninsured banks, with the former prohibited from investing in instruments other than government securities. See Merton and Bodie 1993.

sustain losses, they may lobby for a bailout, and if they are sufficiently numerous to have a significant effect on an election, politicians may reimburse them from general tax revenues. The private
interest and political expediency underlying this result should not
be confused with wealth enhancement or a public interest policy.
Moreover, the actions to limit private interest pressures are feasible.
In particular:

- If there is a legislative body that is relatively immune from the
  pressures of short-term political expediency, that body may
  provide a check on private interest legislation. (We show in
  Chapter 2 that the Senate played this role in Canada in the early
  twentieth century.)
- Regulators should be constrained not to impede the flow of
  accurate information about the financial affairs of weak or
  declining institutions; nor should they intervene in mergers
  that expedite the transfer of the assets of such institutions to the
  hands of more effective management.
- Regulatory incentives should promote the timely closing of all
  insolvent institutions, so that the losses are confined to the
  management and shareholders. Losses to depositors in large
  banks are minimized when measures are in place that limit
  regulatory forbearance and restrict gambling on the resurrection of the institution.

Summary

The economic efficiency hypothesis postulates that the fates of competing firms are interlinked; bankruptcy by one firm promotes runs
on other firms and, because of the illiquidity of part of their investment portfolios, the run alone is sufficient to force an otherwise
solvent firm into bankruptcy. In the presence of deposit insurance,
failures of deposit-taking institutions would be reduced, and viable
new competitors for existing institutions should emerge. The gains
associated with lower costs of depositor monitoring and enhanced

stability of the financial system should outweigh the costs arising from the adverse incentives for risk taking associated with deposit insurance.

The Political Origins of Deposit Insurance

An alternative to the explanation of economic efficiency discussed above is that deposit insurance was introduced because it represented an expedient way to provide a subsidy to certain politically important types of financial institutions. In the spirit of Stigler (1971), the political hypothesis submits that deposit insurance was introduced to provide subsidies to institutions that, because of their high risk, lack of diversification, or poor management quality, would not be attractive to uninsured depositors.[15] This hypothesis differs from that based on economic efficiency in its predictions about the specific form of any scheme adopted as well as in its predictions concerning the likelihood of insolvencies occurring and the stability of the financial system.

The political hypothesis predicts that a deposit insurance scheme would provide 100 percent coverage, because any significant amount of coinsurance[16] would discourage depositors from supporting the high-risk institutions that the scheme is designed to subsidize. Similarly, premiums would not be risk rated because, by definition, actuarially fair premiums contain no subsidy. The low-risk institutions operating in the market would be compelled to join because they would not voluntarily agree to subsidize their competitors. High-risk institutions would not need to be compelled — they would join voluntarily to obtain the subsidy. The scheme would be

15 Cameron (1992) explores some elements of the political hypothesis with respect to regulation and deposit insurance, but few other studies of Canadian banking have dealt with the hypothesis explicitly.

16 Coinsurance shares the risk between the insured and the insurer. In this case, it would imply that only some fraction of the insured amount of the deposit would be covered by the deposit insurance scheme.

managed by officials appointed by the government, to ensure that it is implemented in a manner that meets the political imperatives. Regulators would not bear the costs of failed attempts to shore up weak financial institutions.

Under this political hypothesis, the bankruptcy of deposit-taking institutions is not caused by runs of imperfectly informed depositors, and the insolvency of imprudently managed institutions will not reduce confidence in the other firms in the market. Withdrawals of depositor funds are, in fact, *prima facie* evidence of the rational actions of informed depositors. The deposit insurance scheme amounts to a tax on less risky firms and a subsidy to more risky firms. The subsidy will promote inefficient entry by poorly managed firms and increase risk taking by incumbents with large proportions of their deposits insured. Monitoring will, in effect, not be done by holders of deposits with a value less than or equal to the insurance limit. The wealth dissipated by inefficient entry and excessive risk taking will far outweigh any benefits arising from the presence of insurance.

In subsequent chapters we examine, in turn, the stability of Canada's financial system before deposit insurance was introduced, the reasons for the introduction of deposit insurance in 1967 and its impact on bank failures, as well as the current structure for depositor compensation, regulation, and CDIC governance. We argue that the evidence establishes the primacy of political motives and that deposit insurance has resulted in reduced — rather than enhanced — economic efficiency in Canada. We recommend reforms to the current structure of Canada's deposit insurance scheme that may significantly improve efficiency.

Chapter 2

The Banking System before 1967:
Stability without Deposit Insurance

Between 1890 and 1966, 12 Canadian chartered banks failed; six of these failures resulted in losses to the depositors.[1] No bank failures occurred after the suspension of the Home Bank of Canada in 1923. Explanations for this long period of stability and, in particular, Canada's immunity from the crisis that afflicted the US banking system in the Great Depression, have focused on the economies of scale and portfolio diversification achieved by the large branch banks (Friedman and Schwartz 1963) and the creation of government facilities to provide liquidity to the banking system.[2] In addition, it is widely believed that stability rested on an implicit guarantee of deposits by the Canadian Bankers' Association (CBA), which arranged for the liabilities of insolvent institutions to be assumed by stronger banks, the federal government, or both (Bordo 1986; White 1983). Recently, Kryzanowski and Roberts (1993, 362) asserted that the Canadian government provided "an *implicit one-hundred percent guarantee* of bank deposits [emphasis in original]."

---

1 This chapter draws to a large extent on Carr, Mathewson, and Quigley 1994. Readers are referred to that publication for a more detailed survey of the evidence.

2 The *Finance Act*, introduced as a war measure in 1914, provided a rediscount facility for the banks. It continued in operation until the creation of the Bank of Canada in 1934. See Shearer, Chant, and Bond 1984, 311–317.

In this chapter, we demonstrate that the history of Canadian banking provides both clear evidence against these assertions and a compelling example of an efficient alternative to the use of 100 percent deposit insurance. Using new evidence from the stock markets as well as the archives of the federal Department of Finance and the CBA, we examine the regulation of Canadian banks and the circumstances surrounding each bank merger from 1890 to 1931. From our data, we see that when banks became insolvent the depositors suffered losses, but that in most instances the markets and regulators effectively identified weak institutions before they were actually insolvent. We hold that a 100 percent guarantee of deposits would have removed the market mechanism that facilitated the stability of the banking system — namely, depositor monitoring and incentives for shareholders in less profitable banks to sell to banks with stronger management.

Entry Requirements

At one time, banks in Canada could only be established by special acts of Parliament, and therefore the promotion of a new bank was costly and time consuming. The 1871 *Bank Act* established that new banks would be chartered with a minimum subscribed capital of $200,000. Once half of that amount had been paid up, a Treasury Board certificate to commence banking operations would be issued. In 1890, two amendments to the *Bank Act* provided significant changes to the entry provisions. The minimum subscribed capital was raised to $500,000, and for a Treasury Board certificate to be issued, a minimum paid-up capital of $250,000 was now required to be deposited with the Department of Finance within one year.

Contemporaries were concerned that the new provisions in the 1890 act would establish a monopoly in Canadian banking (Canada 1890, 3854–3862). Their concerns proved to be unfounded. The higher sunk commitment required after 1890 did not deter entry in the first decade of the century and was unlikely to have been an important barrier thereafter because inflation reduced its real value signifi-

cantly. Twenty-five new charters and 11 new Treasury Board certifi-
cates were issued between 1900 and 1929 (see Table 2).

From 1920 to 1966, new entries dropped sharply: only five new
bank charters were issued. This was largely because the government
began to scrutinize the character of the promoters of the bank —
putting up the minimum capital became necessary, but not sufficient,
to get a Treasury Board certificate. The collapse of the Farmers Bank
(see Table 3) clearly demonstrated that even the failure of relatively
small banks could create a private interest lobby for a bailout, with
significant electoral implications. A government anxious to avoid
such pressure, as well as the costs of Royal Commissions and lengthy
parliamentary debates, could minimize the chances of problems by
raising the entry requirements. In addition, it began to enforce the
provision that the charter be cancelled if the minimum paid-up
capital were not raised within one year (this provision had, for
example, been waived in the case of the Farmers Bank).[3] The costs
of obtaining a charter and the standards by which applicants were
judged remained high until the 1960s.[4] From World War I, therefore,
the federal banking system was characterized by substantial, though
not absolute, barriers to entry (Shearer, Chant, and Bond 1984, 358).[5]
Consequently, charters were valuable and provided an additional

---

3 Bill 3, 1921, "An Act to Incorporate the Commonwealth Bank of Canada," received an unfavorable report from the Banking Committee because the reputation
   of the main promoter connoted that incorporation of the bank would not be in
   the public interest. The Senate adopted the report (Canadian Bankers' Association
   Archives [CBAA] 87-517-28). In the case of the Great West Bank, there was also
   considerable concern about the promoters. They were granted a charter, but when
   they could not meet the requirement of obtaining the minimum paid-up capital
   within one year, an extension of the charter was refused as not being in the public
   interest (CBAA 87-517-38).

4 Testifying before the Porter Commission (Canada 1964, 114), the inspector general
   of banks stated that the Treasury Board normally required banks to have more
   than the minimum capital and the quality of its directors to pass serious scrutiny
   before a certificate to commence business was issued.

5 Both of the institutions that did utilize the charters obtained between 1920 and
   1966 (Barclays Bank [Canada] and the Mercantile Bank) were promoted by
   established foreign banks, but neither ever challenged the supremacy of the major
   domestic institutions.

Table 2: Entry into and Exit from the Canadian Banking System, 1870–1966

Period	Number of Banks Active at Beginning of Each Period	New Bank Charters Issued		Bank Failures (or Charters Repealed)	Mergers	Number of Banks Active at End of Each Period
		Used	Not Used			
1870–79	35	19	10	6	4	44
1880–89	44	5	6	7	1	41
1890–99	41	0	2	5	0	36
1900–09	36	9	11	5	10	30
1910–19	30	2	3	3	11	18
1920–29	18	1	3	1	7	11
1930–39	11	0	0	0	1	10
1940–49	10	0	0	0	0	10
1950–59	10	1	0	0	2	9
1960–66	9	0	0	0	1	8
Total		37	35	27	37	

Source: Neufeld 1972, table 4:1.

Table 3: Failures of Canadian Chartered Banks, 1890–1966

	Date of Suspension	Deposits	Share of Total Deposits by the Public in Canada[a]	Loss to Depositors[b]	Book Equity[c]	Double Liability Invoked?	Loss to Shareholders[d]
		($ millions)	(%)	(%)	($ millions)		(%)
Commercial Bank of Manitoba	1893	0.77	0.45	0.0	0.60	yes	116.7
La Banque du Peuple	1895	6.87	3.80	24.8	1.80	n.a.	105.6
Banque Ville Marie	1899	1.50	0.58	82.5	0.49	yes	?
Bank of Yarmouth	1905	0.28	0.06	0.0	0.34	yes	176.5
Ontario Bank	1906	12.66	2.28	0.0	2.20	yes	127.3
Sovereign Bank of Canada	1908	11.22	2.00	0.0	3.00	yes	172.7
Banque de St. Jean	1908	0.34	0.06	69.7	0.33	yes	154.5
Banque de St. Hyacinthe	1908	0.92	0.17	0.0	0.40	yes	139.0
St. Stephen's Bank, N.B.	1910	0.39	0.05	0.0	0.26	no	100.0
The Farmers Bank	1910	1.31	0.16	100.0	0.57	yes	155.3
Bank of Vancouver	1914	0.56	0.05	88.0	0.45	yes	140.0
Home Bank of Canada	1923	15.46	0.90	52.7	2.51	yes	146.6

[a] Value of deposits with the bank on the suspension date divided by the total "deposits by the public in Canada" from the last published government return of the chartered banks.

[b] Because government deposits ranked above those of the public in liquidation, the percentage loss to the public may be slightly higher than stated.

[c] Paid-up capital plus reserve fund as per the government return immediately preceding suspension.

[d] Paid-up capital and reserve fund plus payments by shareholders for double liability or subscribed but unpaid capital, expressed as a proportion of paid-up capital and reserve fund.

Sources: Beckhart 1929; Macmillan 1933.

incentive for managers and shareholders in existing banks to avoid policies that carried a high risk of losses sufficient to require the bank to suspend.[6]

Bank Failures

The failures of Canadian chartered banks between 1890 and 1966 are detailed in Table 3. Assertions that Canada had implicit deposit insurance must be reconciled with the fact that six of the failures, including the last three, resulted in major losses to depositors. In addition, in all cases where the bank's assets were insufficient to meet its liabilities to creditors, calls were made on the double liability of the shareholders.[7] Without vigorous enforcement of the shareholders' additional liability, the proportion of failures resulting in losses to depositors would have been larger. We examine in detail the failures of the Ontario Bank, the Sovereign Bank of Canada, the Farmers Bank, the Bank of Vancouver, and the Home Bank of Canada.

The failures of the Ontario Bank and the Sovereign Bank assume particular significance because of the actions of the other Canadian banks, which joined together to facilitate open-door liquidation of both institutions.[8] The assets and liabilities of the Ontario Bank were assumed by the Bank of Montreal in October 1906, with the other banks giving a guarantee against ultimate loss from the liquidation process. On August 31, 1908, the Ontario Bank was formally placed in liquidation to facilitate the collection of the double liability of the shareholders, which was more than sufficient to cover

---

6 See Keeley (1990) for an application of this argument to the United States in the period from 1935 to 1980.

7 Double liability of the shareholders meant that creditors of the bank were secured by both the value of the equity in the bank and a claim against the personal wealth of shareholders equivalent to the subscribed capital. For a discussion, see Falconbridge 1913, 60; and Macey and Miller 1992.

8 This meant that a formal court-directed liquidation was avoided in the first instance.

the deficiency in the assets.[9] In January 1908, the assets and liabilities of the Sovereign Bank were assumed by 12 banks, under an agreement that provided for advances to pay demand liabilities and for the apportionment of any resulting losses. In April 1911, the banks pressed for payment of the amounts they had advanced to facilitate the open-door liquidation, and threatened formal liquidation and a call on the double liability of the shareholders if they were not paid. The shareholders of the Sovereign Bank proposed that they purchase the remaining assets of the bank by subscribing to a holding company the amount they would otherwise have been required to pay for double liability. The Sovereign Bank was, however, ultimately placed in liquidation to facilitate collection of double liability from the shareholders, who refused to subscribe to the holding company.

These actions have been interpreted by Shearer, Chant, and Bond (1984, 304) as amounting to "a primitive *ad hoc* deposit insurance scheme." But the evidence clearly proves that the members of the CBA assumed responsibility for the outstanding deposits of the two banks because they anticipated that the value of the assets in an open-door liquidation would be sufficient to pay the depositors in full. In both cases, their assessment was correct. Open-door liquidation was thus a convenient means of smoothing the transfer of business from an insolvent bank and of avoiding the externalities associated with a suspension of payment by banks with relatively large branch networks. The depositors of the Sovereign Bank and the Ontario Bank received payment in full, but not because of any guarantee of deposits from the other members of the CBA.

When the Farmers Bank suspended payment in 1910, shareholders and depositors campaigned for compensation from the government. They argued that the minister of finance had been negligent in allowing the promoter to obtain the Treasury Board certificate necessary to activate the charter in 1906. This became an issue in the 1911 election, and a number of candidates for the incoming Conser-

---

9 Of $1.43 million of double liability assessed, $1.2 million was collected, of which $601,000 was eventually refunded to the shareholders (National Archives of Canada [NA] RG 19, vol. 482, File 616-9).

vative government, representing electorates in Ontario, obtained electoral support by promising to provide a bailout for the depositors in the bank. A Royal Commission conducted by the chief justice of Ontario found that the statutory duties of the minister of finance and the Treasury Board had been fully discharged with the exception of one minor error of judgment (Meredith 1913, 9); the findings of the Royal Commission appear to have been explicitly written in terms designed to preclude assignment of liability to the Department of Finance.

Nonetheless, as a result of electoral pressure, the Conservative minister of finance, Thomas White, introduced a bill that provided full compensation for depositors in the Farmers Bank in 1914. The parliamentary debates reveal that many members of the Conservative government realized that to reimburse the depositors without an explicit mandate from the Royal Commission would have implicitly introduced deposit insurance in Canada. That would have raised questions about the need for government inspection of banks, and would have led to claims to make good the losses by depositors in earlier bank failures. But because there was a Liberal majority in the Senate, they knew that they could meet their commitment to the Farmers Bank depositors without the bill becoming law. The bill was passed in the Commons, but died in the Senate. During the debate, Liberal senators noted that Conservative members from both chambers had lobbied them to prevent passage of the bill.

The difficulties of the Bank of Vancouver were well known to the other banks from at least February 1914, when it received a $500,000 line of credit secured by both business paper and the personal wealth of the directors.[10] In October and November 1914, the failure of the Dominion Trust Company in Vancouver prompted a run on the Bank of Vancouver. The vice-president of the bank traveled to Ottawa to ask for assistance from the Department of Finance. The minister told the CBA that he was unable to provide

---

10 It subsequently became clear that the Bank of Vancouver did not utilize this facility because it did not have any business paper to deposit that the other banks would have regarded as acceptable.

this because the bank did "not appear to have any liquid assets which it [could] hypothecate [for a *Finance Act* advance]."[11] The executive of the CBA agreed to consider renewing the line of credit set up for the bank earlier in the year and conducted an audit of the bank to determine the advisability of this course of action.

While the audit was being conducted the minister approached the Bank of Montreal for support. He was told that it would

> be prepared to join with other banks in advancing money to pay off the depositors and noteholders *provided* the Bank of Vancouver has securities (including double liability) sufficient to justify such an advance. Unless we embark on a career of something akin to charity, I do not see how we can go further.[12]

Subsequently, the president of the CBA emphasized that, to provide any credit, "it is absolutely necessary that it must be the opinion of [the auditors] that there are quite sufficient assets to justify such an advance."[13]

By December 5, the auditors had reported that there was a large shortfall of assets to meet the liabilities in excess of the likely collectable value of double liability and that the bank must be liquidated. The CBA's records provide no evidence that the minister of finance or the president of the CBA considered any course other than a liquidation in which depositors and other creditors would bear the full brunt of their assigned losses.

In August 1923, the Home Bank of Canada, an institution with 71 branches spread across Ontario and Western Canada, failed. It was immediately clear that the depositors, who had placed $25 million with the bank, were victims of a large-scale fraud perpetrated by its senior executives and directors. Members of the CBA advanced

---

11 W.T. White to D.R. Wilkie, president of the CBA, November 22, 1914 (CBAA 87-517-03).

12 F. Williams-Taylor to George Burn, general manager, Bank of Ottawa (vice president of the CBA), November 30, 1914, and F. Williams-Taylor to D.R. Wilkie, November 23, 1914 (CBAA 87-517-03).

13 D.R. Wilkie, file note, November 23, 1914 (CBAA 87-517-03).

the liquidator funds sufficient to make an interim payment of 25 percent to the creditors of the bank, secured by a first charge on the assets of the bank. Depositors in the Home Bank launched a vigorous campaign for reimbursement, aimed at both the CBA and the Department of Finance. The CBA firmly rejected the claims, on the grounds of the absence of responsibility and the negative incentive effects that the precedent would create.

Soon after the failure of the Home Bank, it became public knowledge that Sir Thomas White, the minister of finance during World War I, had on at least two occasions received information that the published returns of the bank seriously misrepresented its financial position. White's investigation of the allegations against the Home Bank in 1916 and 1918 fulfilled his statutory responsibilities. He acted within his discretionary powers in deciding not to commission an independent audit (the *Bank Act* of 1913 gave him power to do so). But it seems likely that White knew that a competent auditor would probably declare the bank insolvent. His subsequent defense — that wartime conditions necessitated that no bank be allowed to fail — is of questionable validity.[14] The president of the CBA subsequently took the following position:

> The banks are not in agreement with the view that if the Home Bank had been allowed to fail in the middle of the War, there would have been a financial crisis in the country from which the banks would have suffered....[I]ts failure, while it would have been undesirable, in the opinion of the members of the Association would not have had consequences seriously affecting either the banks or the public.[15]

A Royal Commission reported that the Home Bank depositors had a "moral claim in equity" for compensation (McKeown 1924).

---

14 See White's testimony before the House of Commons Select Standing Committee (Canada 1924, 184–185, 188).

15 May 29, 1925 (CBAA 87-518-11). The credibility of this claim is enhanced by the fact that it is consistent with the CBA's actions in respect of the Bank of Vancouver in 1914 and the subsequent absence of general panic following the suspension of that institution.

That phrase indicated that, although the depositors did not have legal grounds for suits against the department based on negligence or equity, the consensus view was that White had acted inappropriately in not commissioning a full outside audit of the Home Bank in 1916.

Full compensation for the depositors was not considered because, with losses in excess of its capital and reserves, the Home Bank would not have been purchased by any other bank — even in 1916. Subsequent investigations conducted for the Department of Finance found that an estimated 35 percent of depositors' funds had been lost since 1916. In June 1925, the House of Commons therefore passed a bill that provided for the government to pay 35 percent of the public liabilities of the Home Bank (estimated at $5.45 million).

Just as in the case of the Farmers Bank, however, the Senate's intervention was crucial to the outcome. Its members objected on the grounds that the amount contemplated was too generous and that, since the basis for the payments was relief of hardship rather than any guarantee of deposits or legal liability, it should be based solely on demonstrated need.[16] The final form of the act provided for

- payment of 35 percent of the claims of depositors with deposits valued at less than $500; and
- payment of up to 35 percent to other depositors only on demonstration of special need.

The total of all payments made by the government amounted to $3.46 million (Macmillan 1933), providing a return of 22.3 percent of average depositors' claims. Despite the collection of $1.2 million in double liability from the shareholders, the assets of the bank proved sufficient only to reimburse the other banks for the 25 percent initial distribution to depositors. In aggregate, therefore, only 47.3 percent of the deposit liabilities of the Home Bank were paid.

The cases of the Home Bank, the Bank of Vancouver, and the Farmers Bank are consistent in their interpretation of the federal

---

16 The speech of Sir G.E. Forster, Senate Debates, June 17, 1925, 513–521, provides a clear statement of the majority view in the Senate.

government's legal and practical responsibility for losses incurred by depositors in failed banks. By chartering a bank, the government did not assume any liability for its subsequent operations, other than those expressly stated in the *Bank Act*. In addition, the government was not responsible for losses to depositors resulting from frauds by banking officials who deceived the government as well as the public. The government did bear responsibility for using the powers of the *Bank Act* to investigate allegations of fraud in banks, and it had a moral responsibility for losses to depositors resulting primarily from inappropriate administration of the *Bank Act* and any failure to use the investigatory powers the act provided. Unforeseen changes in asset values, managerial incompetence, and undetected fraud could still result in significant losses to depositors, which would not be compensated by the government.

Bank Mergers

Between 1890 and 1966, 37 Canadian banks were absorbed or merged (see Table 4).[17] Most mergers occurred after 1900, when the *Bank Act* was amended to provide for the purchase of the shares of one bank by another bank, provided that the governor in council (on the recommendation of the Treasury Board) approved. This removed the need for a special act of Parliament to facilitate an amalgamation. Changes to the 1913 *Bank Act* provided that no public discussion of mergers could take place until the minister of finance had given permission for the executives of the respective banks to negotiate. Permission to amalgamate was very rarely withheld despite political pressure to do so.

What follows in this section is our development of a coherent interpretation of the political economy of the merger movement.

---

17 Where banks were absorbed, only the name of the bank whose shares were purchased appears in Table 4. In the case of mergers, the names of both banks appear in the table.

Table 4: Canadian Chartered Banks Absorbed or Merged, 1890–1966

	Date	Deposits	Share of Total Deposits by the Public in Canada[a]	Book Equity[b]	Loss to Shareholders[c]
		($ millions)	(%)	($ millions)	(%)
Banque Jacques Cartier	1899	4.53	1.51	2.00	87.5
Bank of British Columbia	1900	4.92	1.64	4.26	34.0
Summerside Bank	1901	0.18	0.06	0.07	0.0
Commercial Bank of Windsor	1902	0.96	0.27	0.38	5.4
Halifax Banking Company	1903	3.77	1.09	1.10	4.0
Exchange Bank of Yarmouth	1903	0.22	0.06	0.32	0.0
Peoples Bank of Halifax	1905	3.27	0.70	1.44	42.9
Merchants Bank of PEI	1906	0.96	0.18	0.68	12.2
Peoples Bank of New Brunswick	1907	0.45	0.08	0.36	0.0
Northern Bank, Winnipeg	1908	3.24	0.59	1.29	0.0
Crown Bank, Toronto	1908	3.03	0.55	0.96	0.0
Western Bank	1909	4.57	0.72	0.91	0.0
Union Bank of Halifax	1910	8.96	1.63	1.75	0.0
United Empire Bank	1911	1.71	0.41	0.58	0.0
Eastern Townships Bank	1912	18.96	2.06	5.40	0.0
Traders Bank	1912	39.43	3.93	7.03	0.0
Bank of New Brunswick	1913	7.89	0.80	2.79	0.0
Banque Internationale du Canada	1913	0.59	0.06	1.36	0.0
Metropolitan Bank of Toronto	1914	8.08	0.80	2.25	0.0
Quebec Bank	1917	13.55	1.04	3.74	0.0
Bank of British North America	1918	47.96	2.95	7.88	0.0
Northern Crown Bank	1918	17.49	1.15	2.15	31.7

Table 4 - continued

	Date	Deposits	Share of Total Deposits by the Public in Canada[a]	Book Equity[b]	Loss to Shareholders[c]
		($ millions)	(%)	($ millions)	(%)
Bank of Ottawa	1919	46.28	2.82	9.00	0.0
Merchants Bank of Canada	1922	100.53	5.85	12.00	27.6
Bank of Hamilton	1923	49.15	2.83	9.85	0.0
Sterling Bank of Canada	1924	12.93	0.71	1.74	24.0
Banque Nationale	1924	32.06	1.87	3.40	11.8
Molson's Bank	1925	53.43	2.92	7.00	18.1
Union Bank of Canada	1925	74.65	4.25	9.75	26.2
Standard Bank of Canada	1928	83.07	3.73	7.72	7.9
Weyburn Security Bank	1931	2.03	0.10	0.75	9.72[d]
Bank of Toronto	1955	537.17	6.07	24.67	0.0
Dominion Bank	1955	1,632.66	18.46	61.48	0.0
Barclays Bank (Canada)	1956	22.24	0.23	6.39	0.0
Canadian Bank of Commerce	1960	2,239.30	18.77	184.99	0.0
Imperial Bank of Canada	1960	790.84	6.62	56.78	0.0

[a] Value of deposits with the bank divided by the total "deposits by the public in Canada" from the last published government return in which the bank appears.

[b] Paid-up capital plus reserve fund as per the government return immediately preceding suspension.

[c] The loss of equity (paid-up capital and reserves) shown in the last published government return implied by the purchase price for the bank. These figures differ from those published in Beckhart (1929, 334–337) in that we have excluded losses written off capital or reserve funds before the last published government return.

[d] Because the shareholders of the Weyburn Security Bank retained the bulk of the financial assets at their book value, the extent of their loss is significantly understated. See *Financial Post*, February 12, 1931, p. 10.

Sources: Beckhart 1929; and authors' calculations.

Successive ministers of finance routinely argued that bank mergers were only sanctioned to protect depositors.[18] This has been interpreted as meaning that the government arranged for insolvent banks to be taken over to protect depositors. To be valid, such an interpretation would require that even banks with strongly negative equity were merged rather than being allowed to fail, and that should have removed the motivation for depositors to run on banks. In contrast, the bankers always denied that any mergers or open-door liquidations required them to provide a subsidy to depositors in insolvent banks. They claimed that

> the basis of the purchase by individual banks of the assets of weaker banks, and the protection of the depositors, was that the assets purchased were at least of sufficient value to meet the demands of the depositors.[19]

Table 5 presents evidence — provided by share prices and absorption agreements — of the solvency of merged banks in the period after the failure of the Farmers Bank. The purchase price for the banks absorbed commonly provided the premium above the market price that is normally required to obtain control of an institution; in three cases, though, the merger negotiations were used to convey to shareholders information about new losses sustained by the banks being absorbed. The evidence suggests that in no case did investors in purchasing banks think that the banks being absorbed were insolvent. In fact, the purchase prices show that only in the case of the Banque Nationale was the paid-up capital claimed by the banks in their last government returns impaired to a large extent. The share prices of the purchasing banks immediately after the announcement of the absorption terms provide no evidence that the purchase involved sacrifice of the type that would be made with a

---

18 See the summaries of the justifications given for bank mergers, files of the Department of Finance and the Inspector General of Banks (NA RG 40, Vol. 83, File 1450 W456; RG 19, Vol. 2673, File 1; RG 19, Vol. 490, File 619-27; RG 19, Vol. 492, File 619-30).

19 F. Williams-Taylor to T.L. Church, September 18, 1923 (CBAA 87-518-09).

Table 5: Mergers of Canadian Banks: Share Market Evidence

Purchasing Bank	Share Price before Announcement	Share Price after Announcement	Bank Absorbed	Share Price before Announcement	Premium of Purchase Price over Market
Canadian Bank of Commerce	215	215	Eastern Townships Bank	175	22.9
Bank of Nova Scotia	264	264	Metropolitan Bank of Toronto	205	13.2
Royal Bank of Canada	211.5	211	Quebec Bank	106	–9.9
Bank of Montreal	210	210	Bank of British North America	120	25.0
Royal Bank of Canada	208	208	Northern Crown Bank	80	25.0
Bank of Nova Scotia	256	258	Bank of Ottawa	205	24.9
Bank of Montreal	211	212	Merchants Bank of Canada	168	–31.5
Canadian Bank of Commerce	190	190	Bank of Hamilton	150	26.7
Banque d'Hochelaga	144	147.8	Banque Nationale	96	–25.0
Standard Bank of Canada	160	160	Sterling Bank of Canada	94	34.8
Bank of Montreal	247.5	249.5	Molson's Bank	152	15.8
Royal Bank of Canada	235	237	Union Bank of Canada	108	8.8
Canadian Bank of Commerce	296.5	299	Standard Bank of Canada	252	17.7
Imperial Bank of Canada	225	223	Weyburn Security Bank[a]		

Notes: The share price for the purchasing bank is the closing price for the stock at the end of the week preceding the announcement that the minister of finance had given permission to negotiate a merger, and at the end of the week in which the announcement was made. The nominal value of bank shares was $100 for all institutions except the Bank of British Columbia. To provide for consistency, the data in the table express the share price for this bank as a percentage of the £50 face value. The premium of the purchase price over the market price was calculated using the share price to the purchasing bank before the announcement of ministerial permission to negotiate.

[a] The shares of the Weyburn Security Bank were not publicly traded.

Sources: *Monetary Times; Financial Post,* various issues.

forced merger of an insolvent institution. In every case, the post-announcement share price of the purchasing bank was very close to the preannouncement price.

This evidence is substantiated by the private correspondence between the negotiating banks and the ministers of finance, which tended to stress the interests of the shareholders and the disruption resulting from liquidation (the locking up of deposits and cessation of lines of credit), rather than the potential losses of wealth for depositors.[20] In addition, the contemporary financial press was aware of the inconsistency between the data and the ministers' statements about the need to protect depositors.[21] The apparent contradiction may be explained by the competing pressures under which ministers of finance operated. Public statements about the necessity of bank mergers to protect depositors appeased populist opposition to the reduction in the number of banks in Canada. These sentiments required ministers officially to discourage takeovers by the larger banks unless they could be justified as being in the public interest.[22] In practice, ministers of finance in this period routinely used "protection of depositors" as the basis for their public interest case, though in fact their policies were simply designed to remove inefficient regulatory barriers to the market-driven process of con-solidation through mergers.

One merger transaction deserves special attention. During 1921, public knowledge of the losses of the Banque Nationale resulted in a run by its depositors, so that by December of that year its cash

---

20 On the Merchants' Bank, see Vincent Meredith to W.S. Fielding, March 9, 1922, (NA RG 19, Vol. 488, File 619-1). See also NA RG 19, Vol. 488, File 619-2 on the takeover of the Northern Crown Bank, and File 619-3 on the takeover of the Bank of British North America.

21 In its report on the announcement that the Bank of Montreal would absorb the Merchants Bank, the *Monetary Times* (December 23, 1921, 4) noted that the Bank of Montreal offer "places a valuation of $12,075,000 on the $10,500,000 of paid-up capital stock of the Merchants Bank. The directors of the Bank of Montreal are shrewd business men, and it may be reasonably assumed that they do not offer to buy assets which do not exist."

22 W.S. Fielding to F. Williams-Taylor, October 27, 1923 (NA RG 19, Vol. 488, File 616-23).

resources had reached a critical level. After an audit of the bank, supervised by the CBA, found it to be solvent, the executive of the CBA and the minister of finance agreed on a package that would provide the bank with the liquidity necessary to continue operating in the short term. The minister agreed to allow the bank to rediscount commercial paper under the *Finance Act*, with the CBA acting as adjudicator of the quality of the paper submitted. CBA members provided a line of credit of $3 million against the security of government bonds deposited with them. In addition, the CBA executive agreed, first, to support the statement submitted by the bank's new management, which showed that its capital and $400,000 reserve fund were intact — but with a note, appended for the minister's information, that current loans included amounts totalling $4.9 million advanced to the Machine Agricole of Montmagny[23] and against which reserves for a loss of $1.35 million were being carried; and, second, to recommend to the minister of finance that the new management be supported in its efforts to reconstruct the bank, so long as dividend payments were restricted.

During the early part of 1923, the Banque Nationale's position appeared to be improving, but more intense scrutiny of the weaker banks following the Home Bank's suspension of payments resulted in a run on the Nationale, which undermined the strategy of restructuring under regulatory forbearance. At the same time, public distrust of the smaller banks reduced the market for the assets of the Nationale by weakening the position of the Banque d'Hochelaga and the Banque Provinciale du Canada; this made liquidation or a division of its branches among the anglophone banks operating in Quebec the most likely consequence of a suspension of payment. The Quebec government was thus prompted to make a takeover by the

---

23 This company had been promoted during World War I, and loans associated with it represented the largest component of the losses of the Banque Nationale. The bank had, in addition, been active in promoting the purchase of Machine Agricole bonds among its customers (*Montreal Gazette*, January 2, 1924). The "current" status of the Machine Agricole loans was justified by the possibility that the company might be resurrected with provincial government support.

Hochelaga feasible by issuing $15 million in bonds, which were used to provide it with a 40-year loan, bearing interest at 5 percent.

The risk borne by the Quebec government represented a subsidy to the bank, but its precise value is difficult to calculate. This must be offset against the costs of the new bank's paying out the $680,000 in (worthless) Machine Agricole bonds held by the public — a condition of the government's financial support of the merger. Any subsidy implicit in the government loan was therefore not large. Moreover, it accrued to the shareholders rather than to the depositors for the following reason: the price of Banque Nationale shares set in the merger ($72) indicated that while the bank had sustained significant losses, in the case of liquidation the capital and shareholders' double liability would have insured depositors against any loss.[24] Consequently, the most important reasons for provincial support of the merger appear to have been the desire to maintain two francophone banks and the claimed links between the Quebec government and the promoters of the Machine Agricole.

The last merger of the interwar period occurred in 1931, when the Weyburn Security Bank, based in southern Saskatchewan, was purchased by the Imperial Bank. Poor crops in 1929 and 1930 reduced the bank's deposits and at the same time increased the risk associated with the spatial and sectoral concentration of its loans. Public awareness of this situation resulted in significant amounts of its deposits being transferred to branches of its larger competitors. As a result, the owners of the Weyburn Security Bank began negotiations to sell it. In a report dated November 1930, Inspector General of Banks C.S. Tompkins wrote that, while the Weyburn Security Bank was solvent, it had been subject to a steady withdrawal of public deposits and, in his view, the management should continue its efforts to arrange a merger with all speed.[25]

---

24 The *Toronto Telegram* (January 15, 1924) announced that the depositors would have lost 20 to 40 percent if the bank had been liquidated, but we have found no other allegations that the impairment of the bank's capital was large enough to have resulted in losses to depositors.

25 NA RG 40, Vol. 83, File 1450 W456.

Over the next month, Tompkins kept in close contact with H. Powell, the general manager of the Weyburn Security Bank, to monitor the solvency and stability of the bank. Powell sought Tompkins' advice on potential buyers, but the correspondence clearly shows that Tompkins was not actively involved in attempting to arrange a sale. And when officials of the Canadian Bank of Commerce informed Tompkins that they had decided not to purchase the bank, he did not attempt to change their minds.[26] His files provide no evidence of any private or official correspondence with the eventual purchasers, the Imperial Bank. In fact, his main role was to facilitate the merger at the political level. His inspection report and subsequent investigations gave the government the public interest mandate that it needed to override concerns about concentration in the banking industry.

The stability of the Canadian banking system during the Great Depression demonstrated that the merger movement had provided a vehicle for the removal of incompetent management and that the remaining banks were solvent, well-managed, and diversified institutions. In arguing that Canadian banks were insolvent in the 1930s, Kryzanowski and Roberts (1993) point to their evidence of regulatory forbearance and their calculation of the market value of bank assets. However, the claim that the Order in Council allowing the banks to report their securities holdings at book (rather than market) value amounted to regulatory forbearance is unconvincing because the banks did not use that provision.[27] Their calculations of market value ignore the fact that bankers secure loans against collateral with a market value considerably in excess of the loan, and that they regularly reassess the adequacy of that collateral in a period of deflation or depression. Some of the banks' customers may have

---

26 Tompkins to Powell, December 29, 1930 (NA RG 40, Vol. 83, File 1450, W456).

27 Order in Council, October 27, 1931. The regulations were operative for only six months: since the banks chose not to use them, they were not renewed on their expiry at the end of February 1932, despite the fact that securities prices did not reach their lowest point until May of that year. Moreover, since the formal change in reporting practices was public knowledge, use of the facilities conferred no advantages on the banks.

been insolvent, but this does not mean that the banks were. Carr, Mathewson, and Quigley (1994) use evidence from the working papers of the auditors of the Bank of Nova Scotia to demonstrate that, at least in this case, the securities were reported at market value and all losses were written off — though most losses were charged to internal contingency accounts. In addition, the stock market certainly did not support the view that the banks were insolvent: the share prices of the Canadian chartered banks remained well above their face value, despite the fact that they carried double liability.[28]

Our evidence suggests that mergers were driven by market forces, not by government or CBA policy designed to protect depositors in insolvent banks. Economies of scale and the increasing importance of superior organizational technology made the assets of most of the small banks more valuable to shareholders of the large banks than to those of an independent institution. Politicians favored efficient mergers because they reduced the risk of bank failures, with their consequent electoral implications. As Beckhart (1929, 340) argued, "[t]he initiative for the mergers did not proceed from the large institutions but from the smaller banks aware of their approaching insolvency or inability to keep in the race." Only in the case of the Banque Nationale is there evidence that the CBA executive attempted to arrange a merger, and in that case, it clearly lacked the will and the power to impose a resolution that did not serve the economic interests of individual members.

The Emergence of Government Inspection

The *Bank Act* of 1871 was explicitly designed to prevent the public from thinking that the federal government was responsible for either the commercial administration of the banks or the ability of individ-

---

28 Double liability would have lowered the value of shares as the perceived risk of insolvency increased. The value of a double liability share in an insolvent institution could, in fact, be negative if the expected value of calls in the event of liquidation was larger than the expected return to shareholders resulting from a liquidation or sale of the assets.

ual institutions to pay their creditors. The act required banks to make monthly returns to the Department of Finance, but made no provision for any compulsory independent audit of the accuracy of these returns by government inspectors or chartered accountants. It regarded the self-interests of the shareholders and mandatory double liability as sufficient protection for the creditors. But at each decennial revision of the act, there was pressure to introduce additional regulatory safeguards for creditors. The government's scrutiny of the financial position of individual banks gradually increased, but its determination to avoid deposit insurance remained.

The chief executive officers of the Canadian banks vigorously opposed mandatory independent audit of bank financial statements of the type that had been introduced in the British *Companies Act* of 1879. They took the view that competition should be left to identify the most effective means of conveying credible information about bank solvency to depositors.[29] H.C. McLeod (1909), general manager of the Bank of Nova Scotia, broke ranks with the other banks to advocate the feasibility and desirability of mandatory independent audits; the failure of the Farmers Bank made his case unassailable. Consequently, the *Bank Act* of 1913 (section 56) contained provisions directing the shareholders to appoint an independent auditor from a list of qualified candidates approved by the minister; the provisions also gave the minister the power to appoint an auditor if the shareholders failed to do so.

While the majority of the banks were prepared to accept a mandatory shareholder audit, they firmly rejected government involvement in any audit. From 1880, the *Bank Act* provided for the most innocuous form of government audit: the minister was empowered to call for special returns from the officials of any bank. After the failure of the Farmers Bank, a clause (section 56A) was added to the 1913 act authorizing the minister of finance to employ the auditor of the bank or some other person to conduct a special

---

29 In this period, the banks undertook extensive advertising of their balance sheets in the press. In addition, newspapers reproduced the monthly financial statements that the banks provided to the government.

investigation should the minister have cause to believe that the bank's returns were inaccurate. That provision was again a compromise between the apparent need for external verification of bank statements and the opposition to direct government audits.

One alternative to direct government inspection was for the minister to exercise supervision through, and in conjunction with, the CBA. This appeared to be a natural extension of the CBA's role, given its statutory responsibility, under the 1900 *Bank Act* to appoint a curator for failed banks and given the absence, at that time, of a central bank and government auditor. The members of the CBA were divided along predictable lines. The smaller banks opposed the CBA's assuming responsibility for inspection; they preferred government inspection if any move in this direction should be necessary. They objected to inspection by their larger competitors on the grounds that these large banks, which controlled the association, might thereby gain commercially sensitive information.[30] In addition, they regarded with great distaste the idea that representatives of the minister or the CBA should have the power to intervene in the running of a private company and to override the wishes of the shareholders. The larger banks, fearing political intervention in their day-to-day management, preferred self-regulation. But the prospect that any coherent CBA initiative would emerge was limited by concerns about assuming responsibilities — particularly the responsibility for failed banks — and ethical questions about legislation; it was felt that market forces should be left to regulate these matters.

The failure of the Home Bank in 1923 made government action a political necessity because it demonstrated the potential flaws in both the shareholders' audit and the ministerial power to call for special returns. The Office of Inspector General of Banks was created in 1924. This formalized the powers of inspection that already existed in the *Bank Act*, by establishing government audit on an ongoing

---

30 See, for example, the reply of the general managers of the Eastern Townships Bank, July 5, 1910, and the Banque Provinciale du Canada, July 12, 1910 (CBAA 87-505-05).

basis and by providing the government with the technical capability to do this. It followed the model provided by the Office of the Superintendent of Insurance — a post created in 1875 in response to calls for a government guarantee of life insurance policies in Canada.[31] Both offices were meant to provide protection to poorly informed creditors of financial institutions, but neither provided insurance: if the officers of a bank successfully concealed losses from the government for a period long enough to cause losses to depositors, the government could not be held responsible.

Attitudes toward Deposit Insurance

An examination of banking regulation in Canada from 1871 to 1966 clearly reveals that the federal government and the chartered banks consistently and strenuously resisted any guarantee of deposit liabilities in the banks. Successive governments adopted the position that public deposit insurance was impractical without a level of regulation that was undesirable on efficiency grounds. The bankers agreed. Whatever gains might be derived from an increase in public confidence would not justify the level of inspection and direction of bank management required to remove the incentives for risk taking and fraud, which would be provided by deposit insurance. Similarly, the bankers took the view that a mutual guarantee of deposits could be efficient only if the CBA exercised undesirable control over bank management policies.[32]

From 1907, a number of US states attempted to establish schemes to guarantee deposits in state-chartered banks (Calomiris 1990; Cooke 1923; White 1983). From then on, failures of Canadian banks regularly gave rise to calls for Canada to establish similar schemes. Support for the introduction of deposit insurance in Canada reached a peak in the aftermath of the Home Bank collapse,

---

31 Evidence of G.D. Finlayson before the House of Commons Select Standing Committee (Canada 1924, 202).

32 H.T. Ross to W. Mellor, August 13, 1923 (CBAA 87-518-09).

when deposit insurance was favored expressly for its ability to promote public confidence in, and therefore promote the survival of, the smaller banks.[33] But in both 1913 and 1924, expert witnesses from the United States testified before the House of Commons Standing Committee on Banking and Commerce about the propensity for mutual deposit guarantees

- to penalize strong banks at the expense of their poorly managed competitors;
- to promote entry by poor-quality banks; and
- to provide incentives for excessive risk taking and fraud while at the same time removing the discipline that resulted from depositors' bearing the risks.[34]

The credibility of the witnesses was enhanced by the failure of every one of the schemes established by US states between 1907 and 1930.

Officials in the Department of Finance believed that neither the policies they followed before 1924 nor the introduction of government inspection in that year provided a guarantee for depositors; to make that view unequivocal, they inserted a clause in the *Bank Act*.[35] The clause was consistent with government actions with respect to the Home Bank. First, it established that the presence of a government inspector of banks did not provide implicit or explicit deposit insurance. Second, it made definite that depositors had no legal claim against the government for losses resulting from a bank failure — even with government inspection. But it did not rule out the

---

33 See, for example, the testimony of J.S. Williams, before the House of Commons Select Standing Committee (Canada 1924, 170).

34 See the testimony of Chicago banker J.B. Forgan before the Select Standing Committee (Canada 1913, 356). The Department of Finance monitored the literature on the failure of US state deposit guarantee schemes in the 1920s and used this in preparing material in the aftermath of the Home Bank failure (NA RG 19, Vol. 487, File 616-23-8).

35 RSC 1927, c. 12, s. 56.15.

government's admitting moral responsibility to depositors for some claim on the ground of negligence.

What Created Stability from 1924 to 1966?

The history of Canadian banking to 1923 provides numerous examples of bank failures in which depositors suffered substantial losses. The failures of the Home Bank of Canada, the Bank of Vancouver, and the Farmers Bank establish that deposits in chartered banks were not insured. The Home Bank's failure also established the precedent that the minister of finance was responsible for the exercise of due care in the administration of the *Bank Act*; it led to an effective system of government audit to facilitate this. Nevertheless, depositors cared about the safety of their deposits — if they had not, the Weyburn Security Bank would not have experienced the loss of deposits that necessitated its merger in 1931.

We have shown that the banks collectively provided liquidity to solvent institutions; however, they viewed any externalities resulting from bank failures as being too small to justify providing support for insolvent firms. The CBA consistently eschewed any responsibility for the depositors in institutions with assets worth less than the deposit liabilities. After 1923, bank failures in which depositors' funds might have been lost were avoided through

- the absence of 100 percent deposit insurance;
- the safeguards provided by independent audits conducted on behalf of both the government and the shareholders; and
- government sanction of a market-driven merger movement.

The absence of implicit or explicit 100 percent insurance gave depositors an incentive to use the information available to them, providing a mechanism by which poor management was usually identified before the point of insolvency. Mergers of these banks while losses were confined to shareholders allowed the emergence of a relatively small number of internationally competitive banks.

The federal government consistently took the view that public concerns about spatial and institutional concentration of banking power did not justify impediments to efficiency-enhancing mergers.

The regulatory structure of Canada's chartered banks from 1924 to 1966 bore some important similarities to a coinsurance scheme of the type we outline in Chapter 4. Because the combination of government and shareholder audits with depositor monitoring was effective in identifying poorly managed banks before their equity approached zero, major losses to depositors resulting from bank failure were a remote possibility. Depositors were motivated to monitor because of the risks they bore, and the actions of the inspector general and the minister of finance were motivated by the costs of lobbying by depositors in failed banks and the electoral consequences of discontented depositors. The combination of depositor monitoring and depositor risk bearing served as a check on the decisions of shareholders and management as well as on regulatory forbearance of the type practiced with the Bank of Vancouver in 1914 and the Banque Nationale in 1922.

Reviewing this system, the Porter Commission (Canada 1964, 382) concluded:

> Competent supervision can provide the public with a large measure of protection in its dealings with financial institutions, although there should, as now, be no warranty that federal inspection would protect depositors or shareholders against losses. Given such regulation, we do not see the need for imposing a general system of deposit insurance.

Ironically, of course, this was written on the eve of the introduction of deposit insurance in Canada.

Chapter 3

The Effect of Deposit Insurance on the Banking System

Deposit insurance was introduced in Canada in 1967, when there was no banking crisis and no evidence of inefficient bank runs fueled by imperfectly informed depositors. We believe that the primary causes of the introduction of deposit insurance were the dual provincial and federal banking system and the tension arising from differences in the rates and levels of regional economic development in Canada. The effect of the scheme was to promote the entry of high-risk institutions and to escalate risk taking by some incumbents. We demonstrate, in this chapter, that the consequence was the increase, rather than the decrease, of bank failures. This adds weight to the view that the introduction of deposit insurance was motivated not by economic efficiency, but by political expediency.

The Dual Banking System in Canada

The three most important types of financial intermediaries offering deposit instruments to the public in Canada are the federally chartered banks, trust and mortgage companies that may be federally or provincially chartered, and the provincially chartered credit unions or caisses populaires.[1] Historically, the chartered banks competed

---

1 In this study, we do not examine the role of the credit unions and caisses populaires because there is no evidence that these institutions were significant for the emergence of federal deposit insurance. This is most likely because of their mutual constitution and the restriction of their operations to the province of...

with the trust and mortgage loan companies for retail deposits, but their products were imperfect substitutes, and important differences between them persist today. Further, trust and mortgage loan companies have been subject to lower barriers to entry, have enjoyed greater freedom from regulation, and, at the provincial level, have undergone less vigorous public supervision and auditing than that applied to chartered banks.

The original Canadian Constitution (the *British North America Act* of 1867 [BNA Act]) contains "overwhelming internal evidence of the conviction that money, banking and credit (in its public aspect) should be exclusively of federal concern" (Laskin 1986, 726). From the outset, the courts took the view that this legislation gave the federal government exclusive jurisdiction over banks. Banking licenses were issued and bank operations regulated through the *Bank Act*. Under this act, only Parliament could issue federal charters for banks. But the cost of lobbying Parliament for a charter was a significant barrier to entry into banking. Trust and mortgage loan companies thus became an entrepreneurial alternative means of engaging in the sale of banking services.

Under the sections of the BNA Act dealing with civil and property rights, the provinces claimed the right to charter and regulate trust and mortgage loan companies. The first provincial charters for trust companies gave these companies the power to accept funds in trust under arrangements that were, for practical purposes, deposit contracts. Federal challenges to these charters were rare and usually unsuccessful. Legal precedents established that firms could perform some of the functions of the chartered banks without actually being "banks," as defined by the BNA Act.[2] The federal defini-

---

Note 1 - cont'd.

...incorporation. In addition, the credit unions and caisses populaires had established "centrals" (incorporated under a special federal statute in 1953) to provide for mutual provision of liquidity and external inspection. See Canada 1964, 155–171.

2 Important precedents were *Bergethaler Waisenamt* (No. 2) (1949), 1 WWR 332 and *Dominion Trust Co.* (1918), 3 WWR 1023 (in which it was held that a firm could provide chequing facilities without infringing the federal authority to charter banks).

tion of banking activity related to matters reserved exclusively for institutions covered by the federal *Bank Act*; these included the issue of notes (before 1934), management of the cheque-clearing mechanism, and the ability to make personal and commercial loans (Neufeld 1972, 297). In addition, the provinces argued that the taking of some deposits was a legitimate part of the trust business and so outside federal jurisdiction (Baum 1971; McDonald 1972).

A potential, but important, competitive disadvantage of provincial charters was their inability to obtain economies of scale and portfolio diversification by operating national branch networks, like those of the chartered banks from the early twentieth century. Legislation was passed permitting provincial companies to operate outside their jurisdiction of incorporation, and the courts held this to be constitutional.[3] This legislation enhanced the ability of the trust and mortgage loan companies to use their deposit-taking powers to compete directly with the chartered banks.

Provincial legislators also encouraged companies to retain provincial charters, by removing residential requirements on share ownership[4] and by reducing required capital ratios. Consequently, some of the largest trust companies in Canada retained provincial charters even though after 1914 it was possible for them to register under federal legislation (and avoid the costs of complying with the different provincial regulations).[5]

---

3 Before 1916, federal officials took the view that only the federal Parliament had the jurisdiction to incorporate a company that would operate in more than one province, but provincial authorities refused to accept this view (Gisbourne and Fraser 1922, 61, 228, 242). This dispute was resolved in *Bonanza Gold Mining Co. v. The King* (1916) 1 AC 566, in which it was held that unless the activities of a provincially incorporated company were explicitly restricted to that province by its charter or by its articles of association, the company could acquire the right to operate in other provinces whose laws permitted this.

4 In Ontario, they were required to have 75 percent of their shares owned by persons resident in the province (RSO 1927, c. 223, s. 14(2)), but this restriction was removed by 1950.

5 Trust companies incorporated in Ontario became important because they were not subject to any restrictions on their leverage ratio, although this was not true for mortgage loan companies...

Until 1954, the chartered banks were prohibited from making any mortgage loans, and only after the 1967 revision to the *Bank Act* did they obtain complete freedom to expand into the mortgage business. Before this, mortgage finance was principally provided by trust and loan companies, and this business helped them to compete with the federal banks for deposits. Provincial encouragement of the deposit-taking powers of these companies was strongest during periods when the legislators regarded the availability of mortgage finance as central to promoting local development.[6] The growth in trust and mortgage loan companies coincided with the growth in demand for mortgage finance and was particularly rapid in the 1920s, 1950s, and 1960s. Their deposit liabilities increased much more quickly than those of the chartered banks during the 15-year period immediately before the introduction of deposit insurance.

The Introduction
of Deposit Insurance

The efficiency hypothesis implies that deposit insurance is introduced in response to bank failures or a system-wide bank run, or to

---

Note 5 - cont'd.

After 1927, mortgage loan companies were subject to the following "standard" constraints: deposits no greater than twice the sum of their capital, reserves, and holdings of cash, and total liabilities no greater than four times the same reference sum (RSO 1927, c. 223, ss. 44(4) and 46(2)). From 1950 onwards, these same companies faced a mandated liquid asset ceiling of 20 percent of deposits (RSO 1950, c. 214, s. 72). By 1970, the "standard" ratio for liabilities was increased — not to exceed cash held plus four times capital and reserves (RSO 1970, c. 254, s. 82).

In contrast, there were no explicit limitations on the deposit business of trust companies up to 1914. By 1927, they were required to hold and set aside securities at least as great as the full value of their deposits (RSO 1927, c. 223, s. 18(4). In the 1966–70 period, minimum capital ratio and liquid reserve constraints placed the trust companies on the same basis as the mortgage loan companies (RSO 1970, c. 254, ss. 90 and 93). Federally regulated trust and loan companies had borrowing limitations similar to those applying to the Ontario mortgage loan companies (RSC 1952, c. 272, s. 70(3); 7 Eliz II, 1958 c. 42).

6   For example, concern about the availability of mortgage finance was the primary issue underlying the Ontario government's consideration of proposals to extend the deposit-taking powers of trust companies in 1921 (CBAA 87-539-10).

the threat thereof. It might also be claimed that deposit insurance provides the efficient second-best policy response if, in addition to instability, the market were dominated by a small number of large firms that were able to extract monopoly rents because of the absence of competitive pressures. The alternative political hypothesis suggests that deposit insurance is introduced to support or promote a group of financial institutions by forcing their competitors to subsidize them. This political hypothesis is supported by the outline, provided in this section, of the circumstances in which high-risk firms managed to persuade the federal Parliament to legislate subsidies in their favor.

In 1965, it was revealed that the financial affairs of the British Mortgage and Trust Company were closely linked to those of an insolvent finance company, Atlantic Acceptance Corporation. Bankruptcy was averted when the Ontario government guaranteed a loan to British Mortgage until it merged with a larger company. The event prompted the minister of finance to announce, on July 5, 1966, that the federal government intended to introduce deposit insurance. When, in 1966, 11.1 percent of public funds was withdrawn from another trust company, York Trust and Savings Corporation, plans for extensive parliamentary consideration of the draft legislation were thwarted. York was incorporated in Ontario, had 13 branches in the Toronto area, and was the sixteenth largest trust and mortgage loan institution in Canada. In the light of these developments, the federal government expedited its introduction of deposit insurance. While the House of Commons was considering the federal legislation, the Ontario legislature enacted a provincial deposit insurance scheme on February 10, 1967, to provide interim protection for depositors of York Trust.[7]

---

7   The Ontario government never intended its deposit insurance scheme to stand alone (Ontario Legislature 1967, 222–223); it was introduced to the Ontario legislature on February 8, 1967 after the federal legislation had passed its second reading. Once the federal scheme had become law, the Ontario act was amended so that it applied only to firms that were not members of the federal scheme (SO 1967, c. 62).

The run on York Trust represented the investors' rational response to a badly managed company; it cannot be regarded as a
response to imperfect information, which underlies the efficiency
rational for deposit insurance.[8] In fact, the key issue in the case of the
York Trust company is that — just as we argued in Chapter 2 — in
the absence of deposit insurance, depositors ran on the company
before it was actually insolvent, forcing it to merge with an institution with superior management before there were losses to depositors. The available evidence supports the contention that there was
no general crisis resulting from the withdrawal of deposits from the
chartered banks or trust and mortgage loan companies in 1966.
Therefore, the need to insure uninformed depositors was not the
most important issue. Of 61 trust and mortgage loan companies with
short- or medium-term public liabilities, only six (including York
Trust) experienced a net withdrawal of funds in the 1966 calendar
year. The remaining 55 companies grew rapidly during that year; the
average increase in their public liabilities was 31.8 percent — with a
maximum growth of 254 percent and a standard deviation of 42.0 percent.[9] Canadian depositors displayed an impressive ability to discriminate between York Trust and the remainder of the industry.

The *Canada Deposit Insurance Corporation Act* ("CDIC Act") passed
its third reading in the federal legislature on February 14, 1967. It
provided insurance for certain types of deposits, up to a limit of
$20,000, which was subsequently raised to $60,000 (see Chapter 4).
All federally chartered trust companies, mortgage loan companies,
and banks were required to be members of the CDIC.

The chartered banks protested against the enacted scheme. The
Canadian Bankers' Association (CBA) maintained that the chartered

---

8 York Trust had operating losses equivalent to 25.3 percent and 19.4 percent of its
   equity for the years ended December 31, 1966 and 1967, respectively.

9 Data have been calculated from the *Financial Post Survey of Industrials*, 1967. There
   is no evidence of the dramatic decline in demand deposits, which would be
   associated with a general run on trust companies. Chequable demand deposits
   in trust companies were $546 million in the first quarter of 1966; $563 million in
   the second quarter; $557 million in the fourth quarter; and $571 million in the first
   quarter of 1967 (Bank of Canada Quarterly Reports).

banks did not require deposit insurance and that they should not be forced to subsidize other institutions that were in favor of the scheme. The association indicated its willingness to participate in the scheme *if* doing so would tighten the regulation of provincial trust and mortgage loan companies and *if* premiums were risk rated.[10] The premiums were not risk-rated, but in 1967 changes were made to the *Bank Act* that were favorable to the large chartered banks and that may be viewed as partial compensation for the requirement that they join the scheme.[11]

One interpretation of the deposit insurance scheme is that it represented a means of transferring wealth from the major chartered banks — which were shielded from competition by entry restrictions — to the trust and mortgage loan institutions. From this perspective, deposit insurance was a competition tax on the major chartered banks (Shearer, Chant, and Bond 1984, 362–363). While the issue of competition and claims of a chartered bank cartel were widely discussed in the 1960s, we think that the evidence weighs against the promotion of competition being the primary motivation for deposit insurance. First, entry to chartered banking was possible. Four new charters were issued in the 1920s — only one of which was used — and one new charter was issued and used in the 1950s (Neufeld 1972, table 4.1). Neither of the two new banks grew large enough to be effective competitors with the incumbents.

Second, between 1951 and 1966, the deposits of trust and mortgage loan companies increased from 8 percent to 27 percent of the Canadian deposits of the chartered banks. This relative growth, and the superior profitability of trust and mortgage loan institutions (Canada 1964, 368) indicates that there were no effective regulatory barriers protecting the deposit business of the major chartered banks from competition of the trust and mortgage loan companies.

---

10 Submission of the CBA (Canada 1967b, 2272–2273).

11 These changes (1) removed the 6 percent loan interest ceiling imposed on chartered banks; (2) gave national banks full access to the mortgage loan market, (3) allowed national banks to raise funds through debentures, and (4) effectively reduced the cash reserve requirement for chartered banks.

Third, we infer from the parliamentary debates and the hearings of the House of Commons Select Committee considering the deposit insurance legislation that the promotion of competition was, at best, a secondary consideration. Introducing the first reading of the deposit insurance bill on January 11, 1967, the minister of finance justified the legislation as a means of "improving the minimum financial standards of deposit-accepting institutions across the country," of protecting depositors, and of stabilizing the financial system. He made no explicit mention of enhancing competition (Canada 1967a, 11672–11673). Opposition to the bill in the House of Commons stemmed primarily from the view that it was an inappropriate and costly way to address the regulatory problems created by low-quality provincial institutions (ibid. 1967a, 12623–12624). The CBA had made the same contention. After the initial announcement that federal deposit insurance legislation was being prepared, the president of the CBA met with the minister of finance and then wrote a memorandum submitting that

> the real objective at issue here is the extension of better supervision and inspection to that segment of Canadian deposit-taking institutions that is not now adequately supervised. The Minister has indicated that federal-provincial consultation would be necessary in working out arrangements for the insurance scheme. Would it not be preferable in such consultation to try first to work out with the provincial authorities an effective system of inspection, since it is the soundness of an institution rather than the insurance arrangements themselves which is the real objective to be attained?[12]

The CDIC Act of 1967 permitted the federal regulators to expand their control to provincially chartered trust and mortgage loan companies while recognizing the existence of a dual banking system. Permitting, rather than requiring, these provincial firms to join pre-

---

12 President of the CBA to the Hon. Mitchell Sharp, minister of finance, October 18, 1966. We thank Shawn Cooper, vice president of financial institutions, CBA, for supplying us with a copy of this letter.

vented any legal challenge to the jurisdiction of the federal scheme. Membership in a federal scheme nonetheless reduced provincial regulatory autonomy, and therefore provincial institutions required some inducement to exercise their option. Nonrisk-rated premiums were the reward. High-risk, provincially chartered institutions and new entrants whose viability rested primarily on the existence of deposit insurance would be the recipients of a subsidy.

Deposit Insurance and Regional Development

As soon as the federal deposit insurance legislation was passed, interest in chartering new banks increased, since the subsidy was now available to new entrants. Much of the provincial and regional pressure for the promotion of financial intermediaries as an instrument of development policy became focused on the banking sector. This was because of the advantages associated with bank charters and concerns that the major chartered banks were not sympathetic to local demands for bank services. This was particularly true for the four western provinces, whose premiers argued in 1973 that the "branch banking system...has not been adequately responsive to western needs," and that the federal government should facilitate the formation of new regional banks, which would

> provide a substantially greater amount of financial capital than in the past to rural and urban communities and would facilitate an expansion of the productive capacities of the western provinces' economies. They would infuse effective competition into the banking industry in the securing of deposits and the making of loans by extending considerably greater assistance to small-scale and risky ventures. (Estey 1986, 365–366.)

Federal Minister of Finance John Turner supported these views and agreed to reduce barriers to entry to facilitate their implementation.[13]

---

13 This included permitting new banks to be incorporated through letters patent rather than an act of Parliament.

The Canadian Commercial Bank (CCB) and the Northland Bank were two of the most important progeny of this new policy initiative. They obtained their charters in 1975 by presenting a specific plan to make higher-risk, mid-range loans to firms and sectors in Western Canada to which the established banks refused to lend. The poor quality of the managements of the CCB and the Northland Banks — in particular, the inappropriateness of their lending policies — became apparent in 1983 as the collapse of the boom in the energy sector sent the western Canadian economy into recession. The combined efforts of the Bank of Canada, which made very large "liquidity" loans to the two banks, and the federal and Alberta governments, which together with some of the big banks provided an injection of funds, failed to ensure their survival.

After the collapse of the CCB in the summer of 1985, depositors rationally reassessed both the viability of the policy of promoting small, regional banks and the stability of the institutions that had been created by that policy. The Continental Bank of Canada came under pressure from depositors; it obtained extensive liquidity loans from the Bank of Canada, but its deposits were maintained above the level of January 1985 up to the time when it was purchased by Lloyds Bank, Canada, in October 1986.[14] And deposits in the Mercantile Bank of Canada had fallen 11.5 percent from their level in January 1985 when it was purchased by the National Bank of Canada. In contrast, when the Northland Bank ceased operations, its deposits were 30.6 percent below the level of January 1985 — most of the deposits having been withdrawn after the failure of the CCB. There is no evidence that the depositors' assessments implicit in these data were inaccurate, or that their actions were caused by imperfect information. As we demonstrated in Chapter 2, in the absence of assurance of full compensation from the government, large depositors in both the Continental Bank and the Mercantile Bank appear to have been instrumental in pressuring the owners of

14 Nationalists made a point of stressing that depositors were misinformed about the quality of the Continental Bank because its assets were absorbed by a foreign-owned institution. They claimed that a "Canadian solution" should have been found (Canada 1986).

weak institutions to transfer assets to stronger management before the value of the equity became negative.[15] When deposits were withdrawn from weak institutions, politicians justified a bailout for uninsured depositors on the premise that domestic and international confidence in the integrity of the Canadian financial system was at stake. Apparently, only the integrity of the policy of promoting regional banks was being questioned by most domestic and international investors — who transferred money to the large chartered banks rather than withdrawing it from Canada.[16]

The CCB and Northland Bank cases indicate that there may not have been a niche in the banking market in Canada that had been ignored by the incumbent chartered banks and that could be profitably exploited. The lesson was an expensive one in two respects. First, the cost to the CDIC has been in excess of $260 million; in addition, the major banks may never recover the $60 million they contributed to the abortive rescue attempt. Second, the federal government set an unfortunate precedent by enacting the *Financial Institutions Depositors Compensation Act* in December 1985, to provide compensation from public funds to uninsured depositors[17] in the two banks. The immediate cost of this legislation was estimated at $875 million, but additional costs have resulted because it encouraged private interest lobbying and implied that uninsured depositors might be reimbursed in the future. In a release announcing the bailout of uninsured depositors, Minister of State Barbara McDougall said that the act rewarded investors who,

> by maintaining their deposits in these two Alberta-based banks,...
> had expressed their confidence in the government's policy of

---

15 The data used to calculate changes in deposits are from the *Canada Gazette, Part 1: Supplement, Chartered Banks.*

16 This was, of course, less clear to the more zealous promoters of Western Canada, who chose to interpret the failures of the CCB and the Northland Bank as "yet another central Canadian effort to 'rationalize' the national power structure, meaning to bring it more thoroughly under the heel of Toronto, Montreal and Ottawa" ("Westview," *Alberta Report*, December 30, 1985).

17 Defined as persons holding instruments not insured by the CDIC and balances in excess of the $60,000 limit per account.

encouraging the development of regionally-based financial institutions.[18]

Similar issues arose when Pioneer Trust failed in 1985. The federal government initially announced that it would not provide aid to uninsured depositors. This policy was protested on the grounds that uninsured depositors had been compensated in previous failures. Saskatchewan's finance minister, Robert Andrew, argued that the whole future of western financial institutions was at stake because any losses to depositors in Pioneer Trust would result in a transfer of savings to the chartered banks.[19] Full compensation was provided to depositors, but, as in the cases of the CCB and the Northland Bank, it is difficult to believe that the decision was taken in the public interest. There was no doubt about the solvency of the large national banks and trust companies at that time, since deposits were actually being transferred *to* them. Full compensation of uninsured depositors was direct subsidy to a small group of western financial entrepreneurs, to the western provinces more generally, and to investors who had placed wholesale deposits in these banks with full knowledge that the higher interest rates that they offered carried increased risk.

Empirical Evidence

The two competing hypotheses explaining the introduction of deposit insurance may be tested using the available empirical evidence.

According to the political hypothesis, deposit insurance was enacted to enable relatively weak institutions to compete with the large and stable chartered banks. It holds that deposit insurance is a subsidy to high-risk institutions and will promote their establishment and growth. With deposit insurance, entrants with inferior intermediary technologies, which would not have been competitive in the absence of insurance, receive subsidies. Incumbent trust and mortgage loan companies may be donors or recipients of subsidies,

---

18 Canada, Department of Finance, *Press Release*, October 3, 1985.

19 *Globe and Mail* (Toronto), May 5, 1985, p. B2.

depending on the extent to which they increase risk taking after the introduction of insurance. Hence, the enactment of deposit insurance should encourage entry. Furthermore, since deposit insurance assures depositors that their deposit contract will be honored even if the financial institution is insolvent, deposit insurance encourages all firms to take risks. In particular, we expect an increase in the debt-to-equity ratio of deposit-taking institutions and in the number of failures. We also expect failures to be concentrated among institutions with the highest proportions of deposits insured, since holders of their uninsured deposits would be more likely to monitor and discipline them — even if the possibility exists that they will get some compensation in the event of insolvency.

According to the efficiency hypothesis, deposit insurance was enacted to ensure a stable financial system. In particular, instability results when depositors with imperfect information cannot distinguish between good and bad institutions. When one institution becomes insolvent, depositors believe that all firms may be unable to honor their deposit contracts and, following the "first come, first served" rule, attempt to withdraw their funds from the financial institution before similar action by other depositors forces it to suspend payment. This is termed a "run" on the financial system, and it may force even solvent institutions to fail if their liquid assets are insufficient to meet withdrawals by depositors. This feature of the market generates inefficiency by inducing individual institutions to operate with less capital and lower leverage ratios than are socially optimal. By eliminating this externality, the nonrisk-rated deposit scheme encourages capital investment and leverage to be raised to their socially optimal levels.

By guaranteeing that deposit contracts will be honored, deposit insurance eliminates the need for depositors to withdraw their funds from an institution. But it also removes the need for depositors to discriminate between prudently and imprudently managed firms, and allows the rapid expansion of institutions that offer higher deposit interest rates because of the higher risk of their assets. The efficiency hypothesis thus also predicts an expansion of the trust and mortgage loan sector and an increase in the debt-to-equity ratio for deposit-taking institutions as a whole. In contrast to the political hypothesis, however, it predicts that deposit insurance will reduce failures by eliminating runs by depositors, and that the proportion of insured deposits will not influence the rate of failure.

Using data taken from the balance sheets of federally regulated banks and trust and loan companies, as well as from trust and loan companies reporting to regulators in Ontario,[20] we have studied the effect of nonrisk-rated deposit insurance on (1) entry; (2) debt-to-equity (leverage) ratios; and (3) insolvency. In addition, we have obtained some limited data on (4) the proportion of insured deposits in different types of institutions; and (5) legislated minimum equity requirements.

While neither item (1) nor item (2) discriminates between the competing hypotheses, these items nevertheless provide an important test of the overall validity of our approach. Items (3) and (4) allow us to discriminate between the two hypotheses.

Entry

Consider the number of new firms established in the 18-year periods from 1949 to 1966 and 1968 to 1985 (inclusive). Entry data on trust and mortgage loan companies incorporated both federally and in Ontario are displayed in Table 6. From 1949 to 1966, gross entry of trust and mortgage loan companies (federally incorporated or provincially incorporated and operating in Ontario) was 37 firms and net entry was 12 firms. The corresponding figures for 1968 to 1985 were gross entry of 62 new firms and net entry of 31 firms.[21] Of the 91 trust and mortgage loan companies that existed in 1985, 62 had

---

20 All the major provincial trust and mortgage loan companies operate in Ontario.

21 The explanation for this increased entry does not lie with an economy that is growing faster in the post-deposit-insurance period. From 1949 to 1966, national output in Canada grew by 138 percent (an annual growth rate of 5.2 percent) and from 1968 to 1985, national output grew by 94.6 percent (an annual growth rate of 4.0 percent).

Table 6: **_Entry of New Provincial (Ontario) and Federal Trust and Mortgage Loan Companies, 1949–66 and 1968–85_**

			1949–66				1968–85	
	1949 Stock	1966 Stock	Gross Entry	Net Entry	1968 Stock	1985 Stock	Gross Entry	Net Entry
Ontario	19	28	20	9	27	22	15	−5
Federal	29	32	17	3	33	69	47	36
Total	*48*	*60*	*37*	*12*	*60*	*91*	*62*	*31*

Source: Authors' calculations.

entered since 1968. Growth in market demand alone may promote entry, but the test outlined in the Appendix at the end of this chapter indicates that concentration declined more rapidly after the introduction of deposit insurance in 1967.

Debt-to-Equity (Leverage) Ratios

Both hypotheses predict that the introduction of deposit insurance leads to an increase in the debt-to-equity ratio. In Table 7, we compare the means of this ratio for the 1949–67 period with that of the 1968–85 period.[22] The table reveals that the average debt-to-equity ratio increased for banks and trust and mortgage loan companies. We also see that the debt-to-equity ratio is larger for chartered banks than for trust and mortgage loan companies. In the appendix to this chapter, we outline an econometric test that supports the contention that the deposit insurance significantly altered the trend in debt-to-equity ratios.

---

22 Debt includes all fixed interest obligations owing by the banks and trust and mortgage loan companies. Excluded from our sample are wholesale firms that do not accept public deposit and new firms that have just entered and that show zero liabilities at the time of measurement in their initial year. In measuring deposits for trust companies, we excluded trust funds. These are funds that are held in trust arrangements, and are not part of the "banking" business of the trust company.

Table 7:   ***Debt-to-Equity Ratios for Chartered Banks***
and Trust and Mortgage Loan Companies,
1949–67 and 1968–85

	Trust and Mortgage Loan Companies			
Year	Provincial (Ontario)	Federal	All	Schedule A Chartered Banks
Mean, 1949 to 1967	10.13	5.75	7.18	22.25
Mean, 1968 to 1985	13.14	16.18	14.22	29.65
t value for Δ in means	2.5*	4.4*	5.2*	5.5*

* Significant at the 5 percent level.

Source: Authors' calculations.

Insolvency

The record of insolvencies provides discriminatory power between the political and efficiency hypotheses. The political hypothesis suggests that, as long as the underlying risks in banking are stable, bank failures should increase with the introduction of deposit insurance, and this increase should be concentrated in new entrants. These results are driven by the banks' strategic behavior. The efficiency hypothesis submits that, as long as the underlying risks in banking are stable, bank failures should be reduced with the introduction of deposit insurance, and any failures should be random across incumbents and new entrants.

Consider first the control period, 1949 to 1966, during which there were no failures of banks or trust and mortgage loan companies.[23] Consider next the experimental period, 1968 to 1985, during which 22 institutions failed; 17 of these, incorporated either federally

23 This lack of failure, coupled with the observations on entry from Table 6, indicates that 25 trust and mortgage loan companies were wound up voluntarily or merged during this period. These mergers were not arranged by the federal government. In contrast to the United States, Canada did not follow a policy of merging failing institutions up to 1985.

or in Ontario, are in our sample (the others were incorporated in provinces not included in our sample). Of these 17, 14 were incorporated after 1967 and only 3 before.[24] This evidence contradicts the predictions of the efficiency theory. The incumbent chartered banks subsidized the trust and mortgage loan sector, particularly entrants that exploited their opportunity to engage in fraudulent or imprudent investment activity. Provincial participation in the Canadian deposit insurance plan when it was introduced in 1967 reinforces this conclusion. The fact that all the provinces except Quebec subsequently required institutions under their jurisdiction to join reveals that the gain in the value of the subsidy for these firms outweighed any loss of autonomy from the substitution of federal for local regulatory standards.

Could this increase in the number of bank failures between 1968 and 1985 be explained by (1) increased volatility in the growth of the real sector of the economy, (2) increased volatility in interest rates, or (3) lower barriers to entry?

Consider the first possibility. The standard deviation of real output growth in the period before deposit insurance was 2.68 percent; the same standard deviation in the period after the introduction of deposit insurance was 2.67 percent, indicating no change.

Consider the second possibility. Interest rates were both high and volatile between the late 1960s and the early 1980s. In the absence of deposit insurance, banks eliminated interest risk by matching the

---

24 The 14 failed firms that were incorporated after 1967 are listed with their date of failure preceding their name — or names, when several failed in the same year — and their date of incorporation (recorded as the year in which the company first appeared in the regulators' annual report) after their name. 1980: Astra Trust (1976); 1983: Greymac Trust (1981), Seaway Trust (1978), Fidelity Trust (1972), Amic Mortgage (1976); 1984: Northguard Mortgage (1977); 1985: Pioneer Trust (1974), Western Capital Trust (1979), London Loan Ltd. (1977), Continental Trust (1973), Canadian Commercial Bank (1976), Canadian Commercial Bank Mortgage (1977), Northland Bank (1977); 1986: Bank of British Columbia (1968). The CDIC negotiated the sale of the Bank of British Columbia as a going concern to the Hongkong and Shanghai Banking Corporation in 1986. Fidelity Trust was originally incorporated as a provincial trust in 1909; it was reincorporated as a federal trust in 1972 and, therefore, is counted as an entrant in 1972.

AUGUSTANA LIBRARY
UNIVERSITY OF ALBERTA

term to maturity of their assets and their liabilities. Nonrisk-rated deposit insurance reduces the costs of insolvency and so reduces the incentive to match assets with liabilities. High and volatile interest rates accompanied by deposit insurance, therefore, will increase the number of bank failures.

The effect of the third possibility — lower barriers to entry — is similarly endogenous to the introduction of deposit insurance.[25] Without deposit insurance, banks that follow high-risk lending strategies or have poor quality management would not be able to attract depositors. Only with deposit insurance are high-risk or poorly managed banks able to attract deposits and grow to a size where their eventual failure has major economic and political implications.

None of the large chartered banks has been so strongly affected by moral hazard that it has become insolvent. This is partly because the business of chartered banks is geared to relatively low-risk loans, and it is costly for them to seek out new customers and design procedures to take on the high-risk operations being pursued by their competitors. More important, however, is that the big banks have a much smaller percentage of their deposits insured than do their competitors.

Proportion of Insured Deposits

We estimate that chartered banks operating in Canada have an average of 48 percent of their deposits covered by deposit insurance.[26] The large banks with the highest proportion of international business have as little as 40 percent of their deposits insured, includ-

---

25 Keeley (1990) questions the long time lag between the introduction of US deposit insurance and the increase in default risk. Keeley's explanation is that entry barriers made existing bank charters valuable and that valuable charters constituted a bond. While elimination of the entry barriers promoted bank entry and competition, it also reduced the value of the outstanding stock of bank charters. This belatedly activated the moral hazard problem.

26 The CDIC does not release data that we can use to calculate directly the proportion of insured deposits at each member institution.

ing those deposits insured by schemes in other countries where they operate. Trust and mortgage loan companies have, on average, 75 percent of their deposits insured by the CDIC, but this figure reflects the relatively low ratio of insured deposits at the largest company in this sector — Canada Trust. The majority of the trust and mortgage loan companies in Canada are currently operating with ratios of insured deposits above 80 percent, and for many the ratio is over 90 percent.[27]

The problem is illustrated by the very high ratios of insured deposits in almost all the trust and mortgage loan companies in which the CDIC has intervened (see Table 8). These figures demonstrate the limited ability of many trust and mortgage loan institutions to attract uninsured deposits, which, in turn, means that the depositors who do place funds in them have minimal incentive to monitor the management of the institution.[28] These data also explain why such institutions are more susceptible to the moral hazard related to deposit insurance.

The relatively small proportion of insured deposits in the chartered banks reflects the extent of their domestic and international wholesale deposits, which are too large to be split into separate accounts less than or equal to the deposit insurance ceiling. In addition, they take deposits denominated in currencies other than the Canadian dollar; these are booked at branches outside Canada, which are not insured by the CDIC and may not be insured in the country of origin. In these deposit markets, competitiveness depends entirely on investors' perceptions of the quality of the management and the size of the bank's equity since, in the event of the bank's insolvency, compensation from the CDIC or Canadian politicians is highly unlikely. Consequently, moral hazard is constrained

---

27 For example, when Dominion Trust, a small institution with $0.46 billion in assets and five branches, failed in November 1993, 97 percent of its deposits were insured by the CDIC.

28 We recognize that, for some institutions shown in Table 8, the proportion of insured deposits will have been inflated by the withdrawal of uninsured deposits in the period preceding the intervention of the CDIC.

Table 8:   *Insured Deposits in*
Trust and Mortgage Loan Companies
in which the CDIC Intervened

Company	Date	Total Deposits	% Insured
		($ millions)	
Commonwealth Trust Company	1970	$5.4	100
Security Trust Company Limited	1972	10.3	100
Astra Trust Company	1980	22.9	92
District Trust Company	1982	231.0	84
Amic Mortgage Investment Corporation	1983	22.8	100
Crown Trust Company	1983	930.0	73
Greymac Mortgage Corporation Greymac Trust Company	1983	791.0	93
Seaway Mortgage Corporation Seaway Trust Company	1983	414.0	95
Northguard Mortgage Corporation	1984	28.1	99
CCB Mortgage Investment Corporation	1985	76.2	unknown
Continental Trust Company	1985	117.0	93
London Loan Limited	1985	23.9	99
Pioneer Trust Company	1985	231.1	87
Western Capital Trust Company	1985	78.8	99
Columbia Trust Company	1987	101.3	99
North West Trust Company	1987	727.0	95
Principal Savings & Trust Company	1987	127.8	91
Financial Trust Company	1988	1,217.0	95
Settlers Savings and Mortgage Corporation	1990	148.0	99
Saskatchewan Trust Company	1991	58.9	99
Standard Loan Company	1991	160.4	97
Standard Trust Company	1991	1,240.6	92

Source: Canada Deposit Insurance Corporation, Corporate Communications, November 30, 1993.

by the markets in which the chartered banks compete: adopting higher-risk strategies comparable with those of some of the trust and mortgage loan institutions would be at the expense of their competitiveness in the international and domestic wholesale markets.

Minimum Equity Requirements

Chartered banks facing the prospect of subsidizing competitors through the deposit insurance scheme could reduce the magnitude of the subsidy by pressuring regulators to increase the minimum equity requirement for members of the scheme. This is most likely to limit the entry of firms. In addition, politicians could attempt to compensate for the absence of depositor monitoring by raising minimum equity requirements, especially for those firms with the highest proportion of deposits insured. Data reported in Table 9 indicate that real minimum equity requirements doubled in 1969 for federal loan companies, quadrupled in 1968 for federal trust companies, and approximately doubled in 1968 for Ontario-incorporated trust and mortgage loan companies.

Conclusion

In Canada, public deposit insurance was initiated in a period of relative financial stability in the banking industry. Its introduction was supported by many trust and mortgage loan companies, but opposed by the chartered banks. The incumbent chartered banks argued that the likelihood of their insolvency was low: each had at stake a large committed capital investment and a long-standing reputation for prudence. While the data on entry and changes in the debt-to-equity ratios of banks are consistent with both the political and the efficiency hypotheses, the evidence on insolvency discriminates in favor of the political claim: nonrisk-rated deposit insurance taxes institutions with prudent management and subsidizes higher-risk companies, especially new entrants that have the maximum flexibility to exploit the scheme.

Table 9:   *Minimum Equity Requirements for Canadian Financial Institutions*

Year	Chartered Banks	Federal Trust Companies	Federal Mortgage Loan Companies	Ontario Trust Companies	Ontario Mortgage Loan Companies
		(thousands of 1986 dollars)			
1927	3,623	1,812	1,812	2,174	2,174
1954	4,651	1,163	1,163	1,395	1,395
1966	3,759	940	940	1,880	1,880
1968	3,484	871	871	3,484	3,484
1969	3,333	3,333	1,667	3,333	3,333
1980	2,976	1,488	744	1,488	1,488
1988	1,842	921	460	9,208	4,604

Source: Authors' calculations.

In sum, the problem addressed by deposit insurance was depositor awareness of the high risk associated with the provincially chartered trust and loan companies. Legal precedent and federal-provincial relations militated against federal jurisdiction being extended directly over these institutions. The enacted scheme offered the politically expedient compromise. The policy of promoting regional financial institutions using lower entry barriers and deposit insurance has not improved the Canadian financial system; it has resulted in the establishment or acquisition of financial institutions by entrepreneurs with a penchant for dissipating the money of both their shareholders and CDIC members in undiversified portfolios of highly leveraged and risky lending projects.

Appendix

We tested whether any market-driven decline in concentration was enhanced when deposit insurance was introduced. We calculated the Herfindahl index on the basis of the assets of banks and trust and mortgage loan companies and ran a simple regression of the index against time, with a break in 1967 when deposit insurance entered the market. The results are reported in Table 10. The negative estimated value of β indicates that, after 1976, concentration declined more rapidly. These entry results are consistent with both hypotheses.

While there is no reason to expect a time trend in the debt-to-equity ratio, the existence of such a trend, outside of our model, could explain this result. To test this possibility, we regressed the debt-to-equity ratio against time for the pre- and post-deposit-insurance periods. These results are reported in Table 11. Except for federal trust and mortgage loan companies, there is no significant time trend in the 1949–67 control period, and the "Chow" test indicates a significantly different relationship in the post-insurance period from the pre-insurance period. For the federal trust and mortgage loan companies, there is a significantly positive time trend in this ratio for the 1949–67 period. This trend (and the constant term), however,

Table 10: *The Effect of Deposit Insurance on the Herfindahl Index of Concentration of Assets*

$$Hl = (\alpha_0 + \alpha_1 \cdot D) \cdot e^{(\beta_0 + \beta_1 \cdot D)} \cdot \varepsilon$$

where $D = 1$ after 1967, $= 0$ otherwise

α_0	α_1	β_0	β_1	R^2
– 1.8	0.19	– 0.004	– 0.009	0.86
(– 114.1)*	(4.06)	(– 2.60)	(– 4.34)	

* gives the t-statistic for the estimated parameters.

Source: Authors' calculations.

Table 11: **Estimation of the Debt-to-Equity Equation for Chartered Banks and Trust and Mortgage Loan Companies, 1949–67 and 1968–85**

$$Debt\ to\ Equity = \beta_0 + \beta_1 \cdot time + \varepsilon$$

	Before Insurance 1949 to 1967		After Insurance 1968 to 1985		"Chow" Test (F Statistic)
	β_0	β_1	β_0	β_1	
Ontario trust and mortgage loan companies	11.58 (6.0)*	−0.15 (−0.9)	9.43 (7.0)	0.39 (3.1)	3.4[†]
Federal trust and mortgage loan companies	3.68 (14.2)	0.21 (9.1)	6.42 (1.5)	1.03 (2.6)	2.5
All trust and mortgage loan companies	5.97 (10.1)	0.12 (2.3)	8.11 (3.6)	0.64 (3.1)	3.4[†]
All chartered banks	24.46 (18.1)	−0.22 (−1.9)	28.66 (11.5)	0.10 (0.45)	6.6[†]
Incumbent chartered banks	26.14 (18.1)	−0.33 (−2.6)	31.90 (10.2)	0.07 (0.24)	8.1[†]
All institutions in data set	0.47 (5.7)	−0.002 (−0.22)	0.32 (4.7)	0.13 (2.1)	1.7

* gives the t-statistic for the estimated parameters

[†] Significant at the 5 percent level.

Source: Authors' calculations.

increases in the post-insurance period. Examining the results for all trust and mortgage loan companies leads us to reject the claim that the increase in the debt-to-equity ratio can be explained by a simple time trend.

Chapter 4

Regulation and
Depositor Compensation

*I am one of those who do not fully understand markets, but I think I have learned
enough not to argue with them.*

— M. Mackenzie, Superintendent of Financial Institutions[1]

The statutory objects of the Canada Deposit Insurance Corporation
(CDIC) are to

- insure certain deposits in member institutions;
- promote standards of sound business and financial practices
  for member institutions;
- promote the stability and competitiveness of the financial system in Canada; and
- pursue these objects "in such manner as will minimize the
  exposure of the Corporation to loss."[2]

The legislation provides little explicit guidance on how these objectives are to be interpreted and achieved, or on how they should be
weighted in circumstances in which they are mutually inconsistent.

To facilitate early payment of depositor claims on insolvent
institutions, the CDIC borrows from the government of Canada at
interest rates fractionally over the cost of funds. Members of the
CDIC pay premiums within a range established by statute and

---

1 June 1993, testifying before the Senate Banking Committee, A-24.

2 *Canada Deposit Insurance Corporation Act*, RSC 1989, c. C-3 (hereafter cited as
"CDIC Act").

determined by the CDIC's Board so as to provide sufficient income to meet payments to depositors, interest charges, and operational expenditures. Taxpayers are not specifically liable for losses resulting from the operation of the CDIC.

The CDIC is governed by a Board made up of a chairman appointed by the federal government, the superintendent and deputy superintendent of financial institutions, the deputy minister of finance, the governor of the Bank of Canada, and four private sector representatives (none of whom may be directors, officers, or employees of institutions eligible for CDIC membership). Member institutions have no direct means of influencing CDIC policy or management. Their official knowledge of the policy decisions made by the CDIC is confined to the limited information provided by the annual report and the statements of its officials before parliamentary committees. Under these arrangements, the CDIC is best viewed as a publicly managed, but privately funded, compensation scheme for depositor losses, paid for by a specific tax on the remaining solvent institutions.[3]

These features of the CDIC suggest that its present constitution contains a number of major problems and inconsistencies that need to be addressed when its operation and performance are being assessed. First, the multiple objectives provided by statute may be problematical. The different objectives of the CDIC are potentially contradictory, and there are no public directives establishing criteria for setting priorities among these objectives. For example, the objective of minimizing the corporation's exposure to loss is especially difficult to reconcile with the actions taken in several recent insolvencies, though CDIC officials have justified them in other terms. The problem is compounded because the information that the CDIC provides to Parliament, member institutions, and the public is insufficient to provide for an effective assessment of its activities. It is subject to the scrutiny of the auditor general, but there are no clearly

---

3 Gorbet (1993, 2) suggests that deposit insurance in Canada "is, in fact, a universal social program financed by a specific tax." We agree that it is a specific tax, but definitely not that it is a universal social program.

defined criteria against which the policy decisions made by CDIC officials can be evaluated. And even if such criteria were provided in the legislation, the multiple objectives make assessment of its performance particularly difficult.

Second, the CDIC Board and staff are accountable to the federal government rather than to the institutions that fund the scheme. Consequently, the CDIC's management has limited incentive to operate a technically efficient insurance scheme. No matter how well qualified its managers may be in their fields of expertise, their effectiveness is limited because their actions are not subject to scrutiny and sanction by the institutions that pay CDIC premiums. For example, they may be heavily influenced by the political expediency of attempting to shore up weak institutions and making payments to uninsured depositors, even when to do so is clearly not the most efficient means of ensuring the long-run stability and competitiveness of the financial system. Since contributions are mandatory and member institutions have no voice in the management of the scheme, there is no incentive even for minimizing costs in dealing with individual insolvencies.

CDIC officials recently described their handling of the failure of Central Guaranty Trust as "a triumph for the Canadian way of doing things."[4] In contrast, the House of Commons Standing Committee on Finance concluded that the actions (or, more precisely, inaction) of the Office of the Superintendent of Financial Institutions (OSFI) and the CDIC in this case demonstrate that

> we are suffering from regulatory failure; that is, the weakness of the industry stems not just from the market, but from the system the government has put in place to regulate the industry and to protect savers (Canada 1992a, 2).

In our view, the problems result from the fact that the structure of the deposit insurance system in Canada is fundamentally flawed.

---

4 R. McKinlay, Chairman of the Board of the CDIC, in Canada 1992b, November 18, 65–66.

The stimulus for imprudence provided by deposit insurance and the absence of appropriate incentives and accountability for the officials of the CDIC and the OSFI combine to make it unworkable in the hands of even the most capable management. If we are correct, greater regulatory activity within the current institutional framework will not solve the problems, and we must consider other ways to improve the efficiency of the deposit insurance system in Canada.

CDIC Governance

The framework for governing the CDIC established by the current CDIC Act impedes the efficient operation of Canada's deposit insurance scheme. There are three key issues.

First, the CDIC is reluctant to close down institutions before they are insolvent to the point of probable loss to its members, because of concerns about the rights of private shareholders in those institutions. Depository institutions have private shareholders with wealth at stake, whereas the OSFI and CDIC staff have no personal wealth at stake and are immune to the influence of the remaining solvent institutions whose wealth is on the line. CDIC staff stress that "shareholders have rights" and that it is very difficult to prove that an institution is insolvent:

> If you move while there are still assets in excess of liabilities, the shareholders are going to be very, very upset. To move at exactly the right moment when the scale tilts would require a remarkable, remarkable degree of insight and there is always the hope that things will turn and you haven't got a perfect crystal ball as to how the world is going to go.[5]

Managers and shareholders of financial institutions that are insolvent will always try to hide or deny this state because they know that, with 100 percent deposit insurance, depositors will not run on them. So long as they remain in business, they can continue to pay dividends when income is actually negative and "gamble for resur-

---

5 Robertson (CDIC), in Canada 1992b, November 16.

rection" by taking on increasingly higher-risk loans.[6] If these strategies enable the institution to survive, its managers and shareholders reap the benefits; if the institution simply becomes even more insolvent, the CDIC pays the bill.

For the past 15 years, Canada's regulators, auditors, and insurers have consistently erred on the side of forbearance — the side of increased costs to the remaining solvent institutions. There is no regulatory solution to these problems, short of giving regulators an unacceptable level of responsibility for the management of financial institutions. Only actions by depositors and other creditors who care about the solvency of the institution will provide the necessary incentives.

The second key issue is that the actions of the OSFI and CDIC often appear to impede rather than promote the flow of information to the market. As we demonstrated in Chapter 2, the original purpose of the Office of the Inspector General of Banks (OIGB) was to ensure that the published financial statements of banks accurately represent their operations and capital. It was a public auditor first and a regulator second. The activities of the OIGB were complemented by the provision of information to the market as a component of the competition between institutions. But just as the bankers of the early twentieth century feared, the roles of the OSFI and CDIC increasingly have been to prop up weak institutions and management. The current approach to regulation and insurance, which focuses on protecting depositors, has removed depositor discipline and the market incentives to disseminate information, as well as serving to impede the flow of timely and accurate financial information.

The practice of withholding information from the market is usually justified by the hope that the conditions causing the problems of particular institutions will improve, or by the need to stabilize the balance sheet of an institution while negotiations for the sale of the institution are being conducted. The creative accounting of the

---

6 These terms have been developed by commentators on the savings and loan crisis in the United States. See Brumbaugh, Carron, and Litan 1989; Macey and Miller 1988; Romer and Weingast 1990.

Canadian Commercial Bank and the Northland Bank went unchallenged by the OIGB in the vain hope that these institutions could be saved. The OSFI was concerned with operations at Standard Trust for 18 months before a special audit called for by the Ontario Securities Commission resulted in public knowledge of its insolvency and forced it to close.[7] Most recently, information about the extent of the losses experienced by Royal Trustco appears to have been unacceptably late getting into the marketplace. In its annual report for 1992, Royal Trustco reported equity of almost $1 billion, but by July 1993 its common shares were virtually worthless. Royal Trust published statements of its financial affairs that the OSFI ought to have known to be inaccurate if they were auditing the company effectively during this period.[8]

Regulatory forbearance that limits or distorts the flow of information serves both to place undue emphasis on the regulators' actions in solving problems and to compound the magnitude of the losses if insolvency ultimately occurs.

The third key issue impeding the efficient operation of the deposit insurance scheme is that the Board of the CDIC is appointed by the federal government and therefore has no fiduciary responsibilities to the members who pay the premiums. The statutory objects of the CDIC — stabilizing the financial system, increasing competitiveness, and protecting depositors — require the consistency, credibility, and transparency in objectives and policies that are identified in the literature on central banking and price stability (Giovannini 1993; Laidler 1991; Swinburne and Castello-Branco 1991). Introduction of deposit insurance or an increase (decrease) in its institutional coverage (extent of coinsurance) will raise the leverage (deposit-to-capital) ratio of the financial system.[9] The resulting increase in the level of financial intermediation in the economy will produce short-

---

7 See "Public disclosure best route for regulators," *Toronto Star*, October 13, 1991.

8 These circumstances led the *Financial Post* (July 8, 1993, p. 10) to call for a commission of inquiry into the actions of the OSFI.

9 As we argued in Chapter 3 and show more formally in Carr, Mathewson, and Quigley 1993.

term expansion, but the costs resulting from reduced efficiency and increased instability may take some time to appear. Thus, *ad hoc* increases in the extent of deposit insurance as a result of private interest lobbying may produce short-term political gains, but have substantial net costs for the economy over a longer period.

Direct government control of the CDIC has meant that policy on depositor compensation has been inconsistent and determined on an *ad hoc* basis in response to private interest lobbying. When the Crown, Seaway, and Greymac trust and mortgage companies were placed in liquidation in 1983, the limit for insured deposits was $20,000. The government subsequently passed legislation retroactively increasing the limit to $60,000. This extension of the tax on remaining CDIC members was motivated by the desire to reduce the public costs of adopting a policy of full reimbursement of all depositors. Similarly, considerable uncertainty results from the current discrepancy between the statutory $60,000 limit on insured deposits and policy: while recent CDIC actions appear to provide an implicit guarantee that all deposits will be insured, the CDIC claims that the precedent is not binding.

The CDIC has provided no accounting of the costs of arranging for 100 percent payment of depositors, and it has no statutory obligation or other incentive to do so. The most recent concerns arise from the House of Commons Standing Committee on Finance's examination of the failure of Central Guaranty Trust and the sale of the bulk of its assets to the Toronto Dominion Bank. The capital shortfall in Central Guaranty implied by the terms of this deal is $1.2 billion. The CDIC has, however, also assumed nonperforming assets and provided guarantees against loss on the loans acquired by the Toronto Dominion Bank, making the CDIC's total potential liability $4.4 billion. CDIC staff declared that, in terms of the deal struck with the Toronto Dominion Bank, the net cost to its members — of the 100 percent insurance provided to depositors in Central Guaranty — was $15 million.[10] To us it appears inefficient to give the

---

10 R. McKinlay, in Canada 1992b, November 16, 39.

CDIC executive the power arbitrarily to adopt policies that result in such large increases in the aggregate premiums levied on the remaining solvent institutions. Decisions that are politically expedient, but costly for the CDIC, increase both the premiums levied on the remaining solvent institutions and the uncertainty about the nature of the contingent liability resulting from membership in the deposit insurance scheme. Even if we set aside the issue of full payment to depositors, the CDIC is not subject to audit with respect to the cost effectiveness of its strategies for failed institutions. For example, it is not clear whether the CDIC minimized costs in the transaction involving Central Guaranty Trust, or in providing guarantees against loss to the North American Life Assurance Company when it absorbed the insolvent First City Trust. CDIC representatives have, however, declined to provide the information required to make an independent assessment.[11] The strategy adopted minimized the apparent capital shortfall in Central Guaranty and First City Trust, and thus understated the true extent of the regulatory failure in these cases. But the strategy exposed the CDIC to downside losses well in excess of those that would have resulted from selling the assets at a "spot" risk-inclusive price.

Schwartz (1993) argues that the governance structure should be dictated by the goals and objectives of the CDIC and that, since the legislation does not define these clearly, it is difficult to recommend reform:

> If...CDIC exists to protect insured depositors, there would be a strong argument for including knowledgeable industry personnel...on the board to ensure that troubled institutions are promptly identified and closed. [On the other hand], if Parliament were to specify that cost-minimization is a requirement for long-term performance of CDIC (i.e., reflected in fewer failures), rather than on a "case-by-case" basis, having CDIC members represented on the board would not promote this objective

---

11 Even when questioned directly about their actions by members of the House of Commons, CDIC staff argued that a subsidized sale of Central Guaranty Trust to the Toronto Dominion Bank was the "least cost" solution, but they declined to give their estimate of the ultimate costs of the transaction.

> [because of their preference for minimizing costs in each case].
> (Schwartz 1993, 55–56.)

It is, however, difficult to imagine why CDIC-member control of the Board would not result in long-run, least-cost policies being pursued. This is particularly true for federally chartered institutions, for which CDIC membership is mandatory. The Canadian Bankers' Association (1992), for example, stresses coinsurance as a strategy that will minimize failures and CDIC losses in the long run. The concern about minimizing cost on a case-by-case basis is a second-best strategy, which assumes the current level of political pressure for 100 percent insurance and the lack of accountability of CDIC officials.

On these grounds, government control of the operation of the CDIC appears to us to be inefficient and unwarranted. In addition, government control only heightens the confusion about the nature of the scheme and perpetuates the widely held fallacy that taxpayer funds are at stake in the operation of the CDIC. Since the member institutions that bear the costs of CDIC policy appear to be the only agents with the incentive to operate Canada's deposit insurance scheme in an efficient manner, control of the Board and management should be transferred to them. The public interest component of deposit insurance could be protected by a statutory directive to the Board that payments be made up to, but not in excess of, a specified level. Decisions about how to implement this policy in the most efficient manner could then be left to the member institutions.

Precedents for such a governance structure are common. In France, Germany, and Italy, the deposit insurance schemes are privately administered. In Japan, Spain, and the United Kingdom, the insured institutions have a significant voice in the management of their deposit insurance schemes (Giovannini 1993; United States 1991). In addition, Calomiris (1990) concludes that the common element in all the successful antebellum deposit insurance schemes in the United States was control of the management of the scheme by the member banks.

The concept of a publicly mandated but privately administered deposit insurance scheme raises at least two concerns: (1) the public accountability of the managers of the scheme, and (2) the potential for conflicts of interest to bias decisionmaking and to result in strategic use of the information placed before the Board.

As the literature on central banking makes clear (Crow 1993; Laidler 1991), autonomy of the type that would be provided by private sector management of the CDIC need not, and should not, be taken to imply an absence of accountability for the achievement of specified public policy objectives. In fact, the advantage of autonomy is that it requires explicit specification of public interest policies and goals. Once these are established within an autonomous structure, politicians will find private interest lobbying more difficult to respond to, and thus easier to resist. While no framework for a deposit insurance scheme can eliminate the potential for inefficient actions by politicians, public scrutiny of the costs and benefits will at least be maximized if the scheme is designed to make discretionary bailouts and extensions of the scheme impossible without legislative action.

There can be no doubt that, with member institutions managing the CDIC, some potential for conflict of interest would exist. But precedents from other countries demonstrate that this type of governance structure can be made to work, and in our view the advantages vastly outweigh any potential costs. Since not every institution would be represented on the Board, the individuals elected to it would have responsibilities to the members as a whole, rather than simply to the institution that employs them. So long as the CDIC Act establishes fiduciary responsibilities for the elected members of the Board, any strategic use of information obtained by the CDIC Board or decisions influenced by the interests of any individual member institution would be subject to sanctions and penalties appropriate for a breach of confidentiality and equity.

Fine Tuning and Extending the Regulatory System

Officials from the OSFI and the CDIC appear to believe that any problems with the current deposit insurance scheme can be remedied by extending the scope and more clearly defining their regulatory powers within the current framework for CDIC governance and depositor compensation (Canada 1990; Handfield-Jones 1990). They have placed particular emphasis on three recent initiatives:

- the establishment of a system designed to provide early warning of impending problems at individual institutions;
- the development of standards of sound business practice that define appropriate operating procedures for financial institutions and that CDIC member institutions are required to follow; and
- the power to levy premium surcharges on members in certain circumstances.

The superintendent of financial institutions regards the fact that he had relatively early knowledge of the problems at Central Guaranty Trust as a vindication of his policies and an illustration of the value of early warning systems.[12] But claims of early awareness only increase suspicion that the deposit insurance system is fundamentally flawed and that regulators lack the incentives to deal with the problems of adverse selection and moral hazard created by deposit insurance. In particular, the Central Guaranty Trust failure calls into question both the efficacy of regulatory prescriptions for sound business practice and the ability of OSFI officials to assist troubled institutions in avoiding insolvency.

The belief that the OSFI can assist institutions in following standards of sound business practice and in avoiding insolvency is misguided and incongruous in at least two respects. First, it suggests that regulators have more expertise in managing a financial institution than do those in the industry, or that they have superior knowledge to financial markets in assessing whether continuation or liquidation is the optimal policy for an institution. But the only comparative advantage of regulators is in attempting to minimize the destabilizing effect of the current deposit insurance system on

---

12 See Canada 1992b, at 2035: 72–75.

deposit-taking institutions. Their effectiveness in this regard appears to have been limited, and their attempts to direct management and business policy have imposed substantial costs on prudently managed financial institutions. Stronger regulatory direction of policy and business practice at depository institutions would probably have the net effect of reducing, rather than improving, economic efficiency.

Second, it presumes that the managers of some financial institutions adopt inappropriate business practices in error or in ignorance of superior alternatives. It is more likely that the imprudent policies and practices that the OSFI is trying to eradicate arise largely from the perverse incentives and absence of market discipline associated with Canada's deposit insurance scheme. Regulators often find it difficult to assist managers of marginally solvent institutions precisely because deposit insurance fosters policies that bear a high probability of insolvency. This is particularly true when the firm is approaching or at the point of insolvency, since the owners of the firm have no more wealth at stake. Having dissipated the capital of the firm, they are attracted to high-risk, high-return investments because if the high returns materialize, solvency may be restored, and only the CDIC loses if the borrower defaults. Similarly, regulatory standards of sound business practice are unnecessary for prudently managed financial institutions and uninteresting to those institutions whose managers are actively exploiting the deposit insurance system. Prescriptions for deposit insurance reform that focus on increased regulatory guidance are, therefore, inappropriate and will be ineffective precisely because of the asymmetry between them and the incentives offered to managers of marginally solvent institutions.

Amalgamation of the CDIC and the OSFI

The CDIC is authorized to prescribe standards of sound business and financial practices for member institutions, and has the power to terminate insurance for noncompliance with specified standards.[13] It relies on the OSFI or provincial regulators to continuously monitor and regularly examine depository institutions. These regulatory authorities share information with the CDIC, particularly with respect to informing it whether the operations are being conducted in line with the established standards, whether there have been significant changes in the financial position since the last inspection, and — if solvency is at question — when the financial position of any firm has deteriorated to the point where CDIC support is likely to be necessary.[14] The CDIC and the OSFI have recently formalized the nature of their relationship in a memorandum of understanding, but there is no formal contractual responsibility attached to the role of the OSFI in supplying information to the CDIC.

The traditional view of the rationale for the separation of the OSFI and the CDIC, as recently stated by Gorbet (1993, 13) is that they

> have complementary, but different roles. OSFI's job is to supervise institutions and when they are getting into trouble, to work with them to try to avoid insolvency. CDIC's job is to manage a solution when it becomes clear that an institution is not going to be able to make it on its own. They are different functions, and I think that the rationale for keeping them separate is as strong now as it was when the government made the original decision in 1967.

In contrast, the House of Commons Standing Committee on Finance found that, in the case of Central Guaranty Trust, the CDIC and the OSFI failed to act in timely fashion because "each had separate roles to play, and the lead regulator, OSFI, was not the one bearing the cost of mistakes" (Canada 1992a). In these circumstances, officials from both bodies could fulfill their statutory obligations without taking the action that the interests of the contributors to the CDIC and economic efficiency required. The committee recommended that

---

13 These powers were upgraded and more clearly specified in Bill C-48, an amendment to the CDIC Act passed by the House of Commons in June 1992.

14 A review of the operations of the OSFI is provided in Canada 1990, 583–601.

> [t]he Federal Government should integrate the responsibilities
> for supervising and insuring deposit-taking institutions into one
> organisation....It would be the primary regulator for all insured
> deposit-taking institutions and one of its explicit objectives
> would be the minimization of costs to the insurance fund.

Similar suggestions have been made on a regular basis since at least 1986, when Justice Estey recommended the amalgamation of the OIGB and the CDIC as a means of providing the regulator with the incentive to respond to early signs of trouble.

While the CDIC undoubtedly would benefit from more accurate and timely assessments of the solvency of institutions than the OSFI appears able to provide, it is not clear that amalgamating the two institutions would solve the problems of Canada's deposit insurance scheme. The channels of communication between the auditors and liquidators/insurers of a combined CDIC and OSFI may be just as rigid as they are now. More important, we believe that the underlying problem is that neither the OSFI nor the CDIC has sufficient incentive for appropriate action as each is currently constituted. An amalgamation of the two bodies, without addressing the underlying incentive problems, would achieve nothing.

The evidence compiled by Estey (1986) demonstrates that the unwillingness of the regulator to act on available information, not the lack or lateness of information, explains the magnitude of the losses of the Canadian Commercial Bank and the Northland Bank. The full extent of the problems of these banks was disguised from the public for at least two years by unconventional accounting and reporting practices, which were sanctioned by both the auditors and the inspector general of banks. The inspector general gambled that a revival of the western economy would make the problems disappear. But by the time it became clear that the problems could not be resolved in this way, the banks were so hopelessly insolvent that any strategy save liquidation was precluded (Estey 1986, 15–16).[15]

---

15 There is a vast literature on regulatory forbearance in the United States in the 1980s. See, for example, Romer and Weingast 1990; and Brumbaugh, Carron, and Litan 1989.

For their part, managers of the CDIC appear to find it convenient to blame their failure to take timely action on the limitations of the CDIC constitution and the inaccurate or late information provided by the OSFI. For example, the fact that the audited Central Guaranty Trust statement for December 31, 1991, said it had $240 million of capital has been used to justify the CDIC's failure to become actively involved at that time.[16] While this statement did not reveal a level of capital impairment that required CDIC intervention, it seems to us that if CDIC officials had had pecuniary incentives to avoid losses, they would have been more diligent in ascertaining whether a viable recovery plan was being implemented at Central Guaranty Trust.

Forbearance and the failure to act in an effective manner result when the payoffs of alternative regulatory actions are greater. When a firm becomes insolvent, regulators favor attempts at resurrection. This is because there are positive political benefits from not publicizing that another financial institution has failed. In contrast, the remuneration and tenure of senior OSFI and CDIC staff are not directly linked to their performance in minimizing insurance payments because their employer, the government of Canada, does not have to pay the bill. Consequently, regulators tend to attach too little weight to the potential "downside losses" associated with gambling for resurrection.

The problems related to the operation of deposit insurance in Canada therefore appear to stem partly from the failure of regulators to make effective use of the information at their disposal, particularly in their assessment of solvency. Efficiency would be enhanced by the provision of incentives for the OSFI to make more conservative and timely assessments of solvency, and for the CDIC to act more aggressively in utilizing it. One approach would be to establish clearly defined criteria for early regulatory action and to specify what action OSFI and CDIC officials must take in particular circumstances. This

---

16 For an attempt to justify regulatory inaction in the Central Guaranty Trust case on these grounds, see the testimony of J.P. Sabourin (CDIC) in Canada 1992b, November 16, 55–65.

would have the advantage of creating a framework for identifying liability for regulatory inaction. It would also reduce the likelihood of suits being brought by disgruntled shareholders in the insolvent firm. It is, however, extremely difficult to establish criteria that would achieve this goal and to prove that regulators did not adequately perform their duties. We therefore think that tightening regulation of the regulators would have limited benefits.

Our preferred means of providing for appropriate regulatory incentives, while also achieving the better coordination produced by an amalgamated OSFI and CDIC, is the privatization of the inspection and audit functions of the OSFI.[17] The remaining staff at the OSFI could then concentrate on interpreting the information available to them, assessing regulatory compliance, and acting as a conduit for the supply of accurate and timely information to the CDIC.

Privatization of the audit function currently undertaken by the OSFI would provide for clearer accountability for the information obtained by the OSFI and the CDIC. It would also provide an improved basis on which to assess their subsequent actions. If audit services were purchased from private sector firms, the quality of the services that they provide would determine their remuneration in the long run. Private sector auditors have an incentive to provide effective assessments of the solvency of firms because of their desire to establish and maintain their reputation for competence and their legal liability for the exercise of due care in performing these duties.[18]

---

17 The OSFI would continue to perform most of its current functions and to regulate financial institutions that are not members of the CDIC. This general approach has been used with considerable success in restructuring the incentives of public sector corporations in New Zealand, the United Kingdom, and other countries. Since the audits would not be physically undertaken by employees of competing banks, this also minimizes the potential problems that arise from conflicts of interest caused by regulation within an industry.

18 In 1992, the accounting firm Ernst and Young paid a US$400 million settlement to the Office of Thrift Supervision to settle claims relating to their audits of failed savings and loan associations. More than 20 cases involving US$2 billion in claims against other firms are still outstanding (*The Bottom Line*, November 1993, p. 11). The Canadian Life and Health Insurance Compensation Corporation has recently launched a lawsuit against the auditors of the bankrupt Les Co-opérants insurance group (*Financial Post*, October 30, 1993, p. 8).

With both the OSFI and the CDIC able to take legal action against auditors, if it were warranted, the quality of the information given to the CDIC would be improved. Equally important, this should improve our ability to assess the relative importance of inaccurate information and regulatory inaction when deposit-taking institutions fail. Additional changes would be needed to induce CDIC officials to make effective use of the information that they obtain, but only a major change in the governance structure of the CDIC would provide this.

Market Discipline: Coinsurance and Risk Premiums

Perhaps the key problem of deposit insurance is the incentive for excess risk taking and even outright fraud that it provides and the demonstrated inability of regulators to control this. This regulatory impotence has prompted a widespread search for ways to force bank managers to bear at least some of the costs of their high-risk investment strategies. Market discipline appears to hold the greatest potential to ameliorate incentives for risk taking. There are two means of providing it. First, coinsurance, which ensures that depositors have wealth at stake in their choice of depository institution and which provides them with an incentive to discipline and monitor management. Second, risk-based premiums, which use market information in an attempt to create an actuarially fair insurance contract, given the risk associated with the portfolio of each institution.

The CDIC Act currently provides for some modest element of coinsurance by limiting coverage to $60,000 of an individual deposit.[19] In practice, however, even this small incentive for depositors to exercise some care in their choice of depository institution has been removed by government and CDIC policy. Since the Crown,

---

19 This limit is also used in the private insurance schemes organized by the Canadian Life and Health Insurers' Association and the Canadian Securities Administrators (Sutton and Andrews 1993).

Seaway, and Greymac trust and mortgage companies were placed in liquidation in 1983, depositors have frequently, but not uniformly, been reimbursed for the full value of their deposits (Smith and White 1988). Initially, this was achieved by provincial and federal government supplements to the payments made by the CDIC. But more recently, it has been achieved by the CDIC's subsidizing sales of insolvent institutions as "going concerns," where the purchaser assumes responsibility for all the liabilities at their face value.[20]

Most deposit insurance schemes in operation today provide for some element of coinsurance by limiting the value of the coverage. In some countries, the coinsurance feature is strengthened by proportional payments even within the coverage limit. In the United Kingdom, coverage extends to only 75 percent of the first £20,000 of deposits. In Ireland, coverage is limited to 80 percent of the first £5,000, 70 percent of the next £5,000, and 50 percent of the next £5,000.[21] The United States General Accounting Office (United States 1991, 17) reported that

> UK regulators believe strongly in their system of "co-insurance," which they maintain encourages all depositors to appraise the financial health of the bank in which they place their funds, not just the types of products or the level of interest rate offered.

In addition, it appears that the European Community has rejected mandatory 100 percent coverage in favor of the principle of coinsurance: a directive issued in September 1993 provides for minimum coverage of 90 percent of deposits up to 15,000 ecu.

---

20 This policy has also muted the merger process as a means of dealing with poor management and weak institutions. Institutions looking to make acquisitions have an incentive not to act before the CDIC has declared an institution insolvent, since the purchase price and the risk assumed will likely be much lower because of concessions that can be obtained from the CDIC. This is because the CDIC will be willing to sell the institution at any price that is greater than its expected return from liquidation.

21 Amounts are in local currencies. For reviews of the schemes in the European Community, see *The Economist* December 19, 1992, p. 26; and Giovannini 1993.

The application of the UK/European Community model of coinsurance to Canada has been actively discussed since it was recommended in the Wyman Report (Wyman 1985; Pesando 1986). While it has received considerable support, it has also encountered vigorous opposition. The immediate past chairman of the CDIC, R. McKinlay, argued that it was "unrealistic in the extreme" to suggest that depositors could distinguish between solvent and insolvent banks, and that it was unfair to place losses on poorly informed depositors with small means.[22] However, such a view both misinterprets the nature of coinsurance and applies an unreasonably narrow view of fairness. Coinsurance does not require that all depositors be able to determine precisely the financial position of a deposit-taking institution. The actions of more sophisticated depositors who do undertake monitoring and the brand names of the different institutions provide information to even the most unsophisticated depositor. Coinsurance gives depositors an incentive to use the information that they do have as a guide to their choice of institution, and it encourages individual institutions, as well as the regulators, to increase the flow of credible information to depositors (we demonstrate this with respect to chartered banking before 1966 in Chapter 2).

Analysis of the "fairness" of coinsurance can also produce a conclusion different from that reached by McKinlay. What definition of fairness requires that people who take the trouble to place their savings in well-managed institutions should subsidize those who invest in institutions with higher risks of failure? This, nonetheless, is what the current deposit insurance system does. The present chairman of the CDIC appears more amenable to the concept of coinsurance, though the 2 percent service charge that he describes is probably too small to have the desired effect (Reuber 1993). We believe that the levels of coinsurance established in the recent European Community directive and those applicable to the schemes in the United Kingdom and Ireland represent the range that would feasibly provide appropriate incentives.

---

22 R. McKinlay, in Canada 1992b, November 16.

Subsidized sales or mergers of insolvent institutions do not preclude coinsurance, as practice in the United States shows (Kaufman 1989; Macey and Miller 1988). On the day that the US Federal Deposit Insurance Corporation (FDIC) assumes control of a bank, it estimates the (usually negative) value of its capital and apportions the losses among uninsured investors.[23] The bank is then immediately sold, merged, or rechartered, and the claims of depositors (net of any apportioned loss in the case of uninsured deposits) are transferred to the new institution. If the ultimate losses prove to be less than those originally estimated, additional payments are made to uninsured depositors, but the FDIC carries the cost if the assets do not come up to their valuation.[24] This policy is authorized by statute in the United States. A similar directive to the CDIC Board should be introduced into Canadian legislation.

There is no doubt that those institutions whose competitiveness rests largely on 100 percent deposit insurance (the major recipients of the subsidy in the current scheme) will be unable to attract deposits under a coinsurance regime if they retain their current lending policies and level of leverage. But if coinsurance is phased in with adequate notice, it seems unlikely that exit from the industry will be widespread or disruptive to the Canadian economy. All depository institutions will have an opportunity to adjust their lending policies and increase their equity, should this be necessary to reassure depositors. Moreover, coinsurance is a policy aimed at efficiency, not at eliminating small deposit-taking institutions or entry to the industry. New deposit-taking institutions entered the market before deposit insurance was introduced. Coinsurance would reduce entry aimed primarily at obtaining subsidies, but it would not deter efficient entry.

---

23 Since the failure of the Continental Illinois National Bank, the insurers have not always adhered to this policy. The insurer must have an estimate of the value of the capital in a bank to assume control of it, so the additional work required in apportioning losses among uninsured depositors is small.

24 By contrast with the current situation in Canada, this approach has the advantage of forcing the insurer to immediately reveal its (conservative) estimate of the total loss in the institution.

Events in other countries demonstrate the point. Argentina had both explicit deposit insurance and a high degree of implicit government support for insolvent banks up to 1991. But in 1991 and 1992, as part of a package of reforms designed to end hyperinflation and monetary instability, deposit insurance was first severely limited in scope and subsequently abandoned. The Argentine authorities have gone to some lengths to stress their commitment not to bail out insolvent institutions in the future (Miller 1993). Yet this policy change did not cause runs on the many small banks operating in Argentina. The system has, in fact, been more stable in the absence of deposit insurance.

New Zealand had no explicit deposit insurance. Government ownership of financial intermediaries, however, was significant, and there was a widespread presumption that implicit deposit insurance existed. When the Development Finance Corporation failed in 1989 — imposing significant losses on domestic and foreign investors — the government resisted pressure for a bailout. This established the credibility of the policy of not providing implicit deposit insurance, and there were no subsequent failures resulting from runs by depositors in the other financial institutions in the country. Similarly, the authorities in Hong Kong recently decided against introducing deposit insurance, despite strong pressure for bailouts from depositors who suffered losses in recent bank failures. There is no evidence that the decision has increased instability in Hong Kong's financial system.[25]

Most suggestions for changes to the deposit insurance system in Canada favor risk-based premiums as potentially valuable, and they form a key component of the reforms adopted in the United States (Mishkin 1992). Such premiums based on measures of risk-adjusted capital are inferior because only part of the risk assumed by a firm is explained directly by the allocation of its investments among different types of assets. What matters more than whether the assets are in housing or commercial loans is whether those loans were made on conservative margins over collateral value, and to

---

25 Canadian Press Business Wire, January 12, 1993.

parties with income sufficient to meet the interest payments. At least for large publicly traded financial institutions, market signals will indicate the relative riskiness of different depository institutions at particular times.

Risk-based premiums do not, however, solve the fundamental problems of adverse selection and moral hazard[26] — for it is not feasible to assess continuously the risk of the policies of every institution and to calculate actuarially fair premiums at each and every point in time.[27] So long as risk-adjusted premiums are imperfect, adverse selection and moral hazard will exist, and the incentive problems that currently plague Canada's deposit insurance scheme will persist. More intrusive and costly supervision may reduce some of these problems, but only at severe cost to the efficiency and competitiveness of the country's financial institutions.

In addition to the theoretical arguments against the feasibility of implementing actuarially fair premiums, we have to consider how to encourage regulators to implement them. Appointees to the CDIC Board will be subject to political pressure to minimize the risk weightings associated with any mandatory scheme. This is because any sensible assessment of risk requires firms concentrated in individual regions — including firms that operate solely in Canada — and those with loans concentrated in particular sectors or industries to pay higher premiums. But this means that the largest and most

---

26 Moral hazard (private action) arises when the insured bank represents itself as low risk and then, having paid the minimum premium, adopts a high-risk investment strategy. Adverse selection (private information) exists because bank managers possess knowledge about the riskiness of their asset portfolio that is not available to outsiders.

27 Chan, Greenbaum, and Thakor (1992) argue that fairly priced deposit insurance will be impossible in the presence of private information about the bank's asset portfolio and moral hazard. They show that it is possible to design a scheme of premiums and capital requirements that will provide incentives for the bank to reveal truthfully the risk of its portfolio, so long as there are subsidies provided by flat-rate premiums. They also argue that subsidies based on flat-rate premiums will reduce moral hazard, since the insurer can withdraw the insurance — and the high-risk bank will lose the subsidy.

diversified institutions would have much lower premiums than the high-risk institutions that have been the beneficiaries of deposit insurance. Because actuarially fair risk-based premiums levied against insured institutions would remove the subsidies that are, in our view, the *raison d'être* of the deposit insurance scheme, politicians and regulators will always find ways to avoid imposing or enforcing them.

We therefore believe that coinsurance is superior to risk-based premiums as a strategy for introducing market discipline into the deposit insurance scheme in Canada. Coinsurance has the advantage of providing both a check on the actions of regulators and a means of discipline on the managers: depositors who have wealth at stake will more carefully scrutinize the regulatory process and the regulators — partly through pressure on elected politicians — as well as the managers of the depository institutions. Practical schemes for risk-weighting member premiums are highly imperfect ways to introduce market discipline. In addition, the potential problems of the implementation of risk-based premiums by regulators suggest that it would be better to give depositors the incentive to use the information about risk that is in the market.

Provincial Jurisdiction and Harmonization of Regulations

We explained in Chapter 3 that trust, loan, and insurance companies may operate with provincial or federal charters. This may create an efficient mechanism for competition with respect to standards of entry and other regulatory barriers, in the manner implied by the Easterbrook (1983) and Posner (1992) theory of federalism. For example, the process of deregulation that has enabled banks to purchase investment dealers began with regulatory changes in Quebec in 1985. These forced policy changes in Ontario and federally in 1987 and 1988 (Cameron 1992, 330).

Significant problems may, however, arise when there are federal externalities resulting from policies adopted in provincial jurisdictions. Provincial governments frequently reduce capital standards, barriers to entry, or other regulatory restrictions on financial institutions, with the aim of promoting these institutions — which may then become an important source of local income and employment, as well as credit for small business and other high-risk local development projects. The operation of the CDIC provides a vehicle for externalities to arise from these policies, in that it insures provincially incorporated institutions, despite the variety of regulatory frameworks applicable to them.[28] The costs of increases in the risk of failure arising from strategic provincial policies are borne by members of the CDIC from outside the province.[29]

One approach to the problems created by the potential for strategic action by individual provinces is to attempt to harmonize regulation, so that all CDIC members are chartered and regulated according to the same standards. In our view, however, the tangible gains arising from harmonization initiatives will, at best, be small and short term. This is because there is no reason for provinces to charter institutions at all if their regulations are going to be exactly the same as those of the other provinces and the federal system. Quebec was so concerned about the potential for federal regulatory encroachment resulting from the CDIC that it established an independent scheme (Parizeau 1969, 115).

Provinces have fought for the power to charter depository institutions so that they can adopt policy that is different from that in other jurisdictions. So long as they retain this power, long-term attempts to promote harmonization will be futile. In addition, strategic behavior by individual provinces could destabilize the scheme through the promotion of low-quality institutions that obtain insurance from the CDIC. While this problem is more likely to be resolved by politicians than by CDIC officials, we believe that coinsurance

---

28 The requirement established in the CDIC Act that provincially incorporated institutions agree "not to exercise powers substantially different" from those available under the applicable federal legislation has, under political pressure from the provinces, been interpreted in a very liberal manner.

29 The failure of the Principal Group of companies is often held up as an example of the problems arising from provincial governments' reaping the benefits, but not the costs, of the promotion of low-quality financial institutions (Cameron 1992, 334–335).

will also improve this aspect of the system: depositors with some portion of their funds at risk in the event of insolvency will limit any jurisdiction's ability to promote low-quality financial institutions, and thus limit the payoffs of strategic behavior by the provinces.

Conclusion

Canada's current system of deposit insurance has relied too much on regulators' ability to prevent failures of financial institutions and minimize the loss of capital in insolvent institutions. In the face of the powerful incentives for excessive levels of risk taking provided by deposit insurance, regulators have proved powerless to stop insolvencies and have consistently failed to close declining institutions before they become insolvent. Regulators' attempts to assist institutions on the verge of insolvency have generally been unsuccessful in restoring financial health. Moreover, they have substantially increased the losses of uninsured creditors and CDIC members.

Enhanced regulatory powers and regulatory assessment criteria are, in our view, unlikely to produce tangible benefits. Reforms must instead focus on the introduction of more market-based disciplinary mechanisms. In addition, public officials should be given greater incentive to act in the interests of economic efficiency. For these reasons, we believe that the reforms most likely to bring about improvements in the deposit insurance system are management of CDIC by its member institutions, the introduction of coinsurance, and the privatization of the inspection functions of the OSFI.

Chapter 5

Conclusions and Recommendations

Deposit insurance of the type now provided by the *Canada Deposit Insurance Corporation Act* (CDIC Act) is an unnecessary and highly costly means of protecting depositors. Furthermore, it is a major impediment to the efficient operation of the Canadian financial system.

The Canada Deposit Insurance Corporation was established primarily to protect and increase federal authority over politically important — but imprudently managed — trust and mortgage loan companies chartered by the provinces. The Canadian financial system was stable prior to the establishment of the CDIC in 1967: there were no system-wide runs on depository institutions, and there had been no failures of federally chartered banks since 1923.

By reducing market discipline, deposit insurance has facilitated inefficient entry, provided incentives for imprudent behavior, and protected weak or fraudulent management. These features of deposit insurance have increased instability in the financial system, reduced effective competition for the major banks, and imposed a specific tax on more prudently managed institutions. Failures of banks and trust and mortgage loan companies have cost the CDIC in excess of $3.5 billion to date, all of which must be recovered by assessments levied on the remaining members.

The Rationale for Reform

The institutions that currently exploit or benefit from the operation of the CDIC naturally oppose substantive change. Even those who recognize the net costs of the current scheme often cite concerns about stability, competition, and unsophisticated depositors. Their proposals for reform are thus more timorous and incomplete than are required for the efficient operation of the financial system. Transition costs would be incurred in any attempt to radically change or eliminate a policy that has been in place for more than 25 years, because both institutions and depositors would need time to adjust their behavior. But since the evidence presented in this study suggests that neither unsophisticated depositors nor competition and stability in the financial system justify Canada's current deposit insurance scheme, we believe that major reforms can and should be undertaken.

In Chapter 2, we showed that no depositor lost any wealth as a result of the failure of a Canadian chartered bank in the period from 1924 to 1967. In the absence of formal or implicit deposit insurance, stability of the banking system was maintained through the combination of monitoring by depositors and shareholders, public sanction of purchases of weak institutions by those with superior management, a credible government audit and inspection service designed to curtail fraud, and the absence of obvious attempts to promote regional or provincial interests by subsidizing entry. We believe that the period before 1967 produced a viable regime and one that was superior to that in place in Canada today.

In Chapter 3, we showed the implausibility of claims that the CDIC was established to promote economic efficiency. Deposit insurance increased both insolvencies and the instability of the Canadian financial system. Insolvencies have been confined to two types of institutions: new entrants that strategically exploited the subsidy provided by deposit insurance; and institutions with very high proportions of their deposits insured and that were subject to little depositor monitoring. In both cases, the underlying causes of the problem are likely the loss of market discipline and the incentive for financial entrepreneurs to dissipate the money of shareholders and the CDIC members in undiversified and high-risk loan portfolios, which are associated with deposit insurance.

Supporters of Canada's current deposit insurance scheme hold that it is instrumental in fostering competition with the chartered banks. We agree that competition is valuable; we support the growth of a viable, independent trust and mortgage loan sector so long as there is a market for its services; and we believe that any regulations that restrict nonbank deposit-taking institutions in competing directly with banks or in having banking subsidiaries should be removed. But the evidence clearly indicates that deposit insurance has failed either to compensate for regulatory impediments to competition or to subsidize the growth of competitive firms. The incentive for imprudence provided by deposit insurance has outweighed any of the claimed beneficial effects and has reduced, rather than increased, the number of viable and independent competitors for the large chartered banks.

The arguments of those who defend the current deposit insurance scheme have also been undermined by recent innovations in the financial services sector, which have dramatically increased the accessibility of mutual funds invested largely or entirely in treasury bills and government bonds. These liquid and low-risk investment instruments are now widely available in small denominations. The existence of market instruments that provide an efficient vehicle for unsophisticated depositors and those averse to risk highlights the unnecessary distortion in investment patterns arising from deposit insurance.

The approaches to reform advocated by the CDIC and the Office of the Superintendent of Financial Institutions (OSFI) involve increasing control over the management of deposit-taking institutions, instituting new and more complex evaluation criteria to guide regulatory activities, and hiring more regulators. The increasing tendency toward managing deposit-taking institutions by regulators is inappropriate. In contrast to shareholders and managers of financial institutions, regulators lack both the practical knowledge and the pecuniary incentives required for effective management. As Adam Smith noted, regulatory direction of business activity "would no-where be so dangerous as in the hands of a man who had folly and presumption enough to fancy himself fit to exercise it" (Smith [1776] 1976, vol. 1, 478). The increasing specificity of regulations may not only inhibit efficiency and stifle entrepreneurship, but also lead to regulatory inaction by substituting accounting benchmarks for the exercise of judgment. Recent history has not shown that the proliferation of regulations and regulatory authority provides any tangible economy-wide benefits — although it may serve to provide private benefits for favored groups of institutions and improve the career prospects of financial sector regulators.

Compensation of Depositors

The key problems arising from the current CDIC policy on depositor compensation are twofold: the elimination of the incentive for depositor monitoring resulting from 100 percent coverage up to the limit of $60,000, and the uncertainty created by inconsistent policy with respect to coverage above that level. The most effective reform strategy would be the introduction of coinsurance at a level that would reintroduce the type of market discipline that prevailed in Canada before 1967. This would require a significant reduction in the coverage of deposit insurance, and we consider that a reasonable maximum limit of such coverage would be 80 percent. This reduction in coverage should be phased in over a limited time period — such as two years — to allow depositors and institutions to adjust to the new environment. We therefore recommend the following:

- The coverage provided by the CDIC should be reduced, over a period of two years by four steps of 5 percent each, to 80 percent of the first $60,000 of a deposit.
- When insolvent institutions are sold as going concerns, coinsurance should be enforced by the apportioning of losses to insured and uninsured deposit accounts — as is done in the United States. The CDIC Act should contain an explicit directive to the CDIC Board to this effect.

Coinsurance does not require that all depositors be able to determine precisely the financial position of a deposit-taking institution. It gives depositors an incentive to use the information that they do have when placing a deposit, and it encourages individual institutions, as well as the regulators, to increase the flow of credible information to depositors.

Constitution and Governance of the CDIC

Two key features of the constitution and governance of the CDIC inhibit its performance and are contrary to the objective of promoting an efficient and competitive financial system: the lack of accountability of the CDIC Board and management to the institutions that pay the premium income and have wealth at stake in the scheme; and compulsory membership.

Governance of the CDIC

CDIC staff are insulated from scrutiny or sanction by the institutions that pay the premium income. The potential inefficiencies resulting from this situation could be ameliorated to some extent by CDIC member institutions being given the right to employ auditors to assess the actions of CDIC staff. We take the view, however, that the principle of management by the institutions with wealth at stake must be achieved more directly and through more substantial reforms. Specifically:

- The CDIC should be reconstituted with the member institutions as shareholders.
- The CDIC should be managed by a Board elected from its shareholders, with appropriate allowance for representation of different types of institutions.
- The CDIC Act should establish fiduciary responsibilities for the elected members of the Board. Any strategic use of information obtained in the CDIC Board or decisionmaking dictated by the

interests of any individual member institution should be subject to sanctions and penalties appropriate for breach of confidentiality and equity.

- The conditions of CDIC membership should clearly establish grounds for the closure of an institution, thus limiting the exposure of the CDIC Board to lawsuits from shareholders in marginally insolvent institutions.
- The CDIC's actions should be made publicly accountable through a legislative directive on the compensation of depositors and through the appointment of one member of the Board.

Membership of the CDIC

If, in the presence of imperfect information, a deposit insurance scheme is required to stabilize the financial system, all institutions will benefit from its introduction and will join a soundly managed scheme voluntarily. But if, as we argued in Chapter 3, the scheme is designed to provide a subsidy to politically important but imprudently managed institutions, compulsory membership is an unwarranted tax on prudence and efficiency. In the first case, compulsory membership is illogical; in the second case, it is unjustifiable. Making membership voluntary would highlight the primacy of the political motivation for Canada's deposit insurance scheme and spur the quest for more efficient means of providing low-risk savings instruments for unsophisticated depositors. Voluntary membership would also promote the competitiveness and stability of the financial system. We therefore recommend the following:

- When the coinsurance ratio of 80 percent is reached (after two years), membership of the CDIC should become voluntary. Voluntary membership has the virtue of providing a framework within which the managers, shareholders, and depositors in individual financial institutions ultimately may decide whether deposit insurance needs to be retained at all.
- Depositors with uninsured banks should be required to sign a statement acknowledging that they have been informed that

their deposits are not insured by the CDIC or the government of Canada (as is currently required for purchases of mutual funds).

The Relationship between the OSFI and the CDIC

The OSFI and the CDIC share a twofold weakness: the lack of incentives to make timely and accurate assessments of the solvency of financial institutions, and their lack of accountability for their diligence in obtaining and providing information. Amalgamating the two institutions would not resolve these problems and might make them worse. The OSFI should focus on ensuring that the CDIC receives accurate and timely information on the solvency of its members. The relationship between the OSFI and the institutions that it regulates should be at arm's length to avoid the compromise that arises when the regulator attempts to work with and support weak institutions. We therefore recommend the following:

- The OSFI and the CDIC should continue to be separate institutions.
- The inspection and audit services now provided by the OSFI should be privatized; the OSFI should purchase these services from the most effective supplier when they are required to supplement market information and statutory returns.
- Information on the solvency of individual institutions purchased or obtained by the OSFI should be sold to the CDIC at a nominal cost, to establish a legally binding contract for the exercise of due diligence by the OSFI and the auditors with which it contracts.

Effects of Our Recommendations

Coinsurance in the form set out above would encourage closer private and public sector scrutiny of the accuracy of returns provided by financial intermediaries, while still providing a substantial degree of protection for depositors. By thus reducing the potential for moral hazard that is associated with deposit insurance and making it more difficult for uncompetitive firms to become established in the industry, coinsurance would have the effect of reducing the incidence of insolvency. Should any institutions reach the point of insolvency, depositors with wealth at risk would play a vital role in disciplining the subsequent actions of management and regulators. Coinsurance would also increase the demand for public information on the solvency of banks and trust companies, and encourage these institutions to compete for deposits through the dissemination of this information.

The proposed governance structure for the CDIC would improve efficiency by giving management and decisionmaking powers to the agents who have wealth at stake in the scheme. This should improve the timeliness of the CDIC's actions and ensure that it adopts a long-term minimum-cost management strategy. With the provision and flow of information from the OSFI to the CDIC on a contractual basis, the officials in the OSFI and CDIC would be unable to deflect scrutiny of their actions and the information on which they were based. This arrangement would also give the CDIC legal recourse for negligence in the supply of information by the OSFI or the auditors it employs. The flow of accurate information to the market should be increased by the sanctions for regulatory forbearance that this system would provide.

Finally, we expect our recommendations to improve the overall performance of the Canadian economy. The dissipation of wealth and misallocation of resources caused by the current deposit insurance scheme should be substantially reduced. Our recommendations would both promote the domestic and international competitiveness of Canada's financial intermediaries, and give them significant advantages over firms based in the increasingly stifling regulatory environment of the United States.

References

Baum, D.J. 1971. "The Near Banks: Trust Companies of Canada," *Tulane Law Review* 45: 546–571.

Beckhart, B.H. 1929. "The Banking System of Canada." In *Foreign Banking Systems*, edited by H.P. Willis and B.H. Beckhart. New York: Henry Holt.

Bernanke, B.S. 1983. "Non-Monetary Effects of the Financial Crisis in the Propagation of the Great Depression," *American Economic Review* 73: 257–276.

Binhammer, H. and J. Boulakia. 1968. "Deposit Insurance In Canada," *Canadian Banker* 75: 38–44.

Bordo, M.D. 1986. "Financial Crises, Banking Crises, Stock Market Crashes, and the Money Supply: Some International Evidence, 1870–1933." In *Financial Crises and World Banking Systems*, edited by F. Capie and G.E. Wood. New York: St. Martin's Press.

Brumbaugh, R.D. Jr., A.S. Carron, and R.E. Litan. 1989. "Cleaning Up the Depository Institutions Mess," *Brookings Papers on Economic Activity* (1): 243–283.

Calomiris, C.W. 1990. "Is Deposit Insurance Necessary? A Historical Perspective," *Journal of Economic History* 50: 283–295.

Cameron, N.E. 1992. *Money, Financial Markets, and Economic Activity*, 2d ed. Don Mills, Ont.: Addison Wesley.

Canada. 1890. House of Commons. *Debates*. Ottawa.

————. 1913. House of Commons. Select Standing Committee on Banking and Commerce. *Proceedings*. Ottawa.

————. 1924. House of Commons. Select Standing Committee on Banking and Commerce. *Proceedings*. Ottawa.

————. 1964. Royal Commission on Banking and Finance (Porter Commission). *Report*. Ottawa: Queen's Printer.

————. 1967a. House of Commons. *Debates*. Ottawa.

————. 1967b. House of Commons. *Hearings of the Standing Committee of the Canadian House of Commons on Finance*. Ottawa: Queen's Printer.

———. 1986. House of Commons. *Report of the Standing Committee on Finance and Economic Affairs*, December 10.

———. 1990. Auditor General. "Office of the Superintendent of Financial Institutions" in *Report of the Auditor General of Canada to the House of Commons*. Ottawa: Government Printer.

———. 1992a. House of Commons. Standing Committee on Finance. *Sixteenth Report*. Ottawa.

———. 1992b. House of Commons. Standing Committee on Finance. Subcommittee on Financial Institutions. *Transcript of Committee Proceedings*. Ottawa, November 16–18.

———. 1993. Senate. Standing Committee on Banking. *Proceedings*. Ottawa.

Canada Deposit Insurance Corporation. 1991. *Annual Report*. Toronto.

Canadian Bankers' Association. 1992. "Deposit Insurance Reform: Needed Improvements to Ensure Competitiveness of Canada's Financial Institutions." Paper submitted to the Minister of State, Finance and Privatization. Toronto.

Carr, J., G.F. Mathewson, and N.C. Quigley. 1993. "Political and Efficiency Motives for Deposit Insurance." University of Toronto. Institute for Policy Analysis. Mimeographed.

———, G.F. Mathewson, and N.C. Quigley. 1994. "Stability in the Absence of Deposit Insurance: Canadian Banking, 1890–1966," Working Paper. University of Toronto. Institute for Policy Analysis.

Chan, Y., S.I. Greenbaum, and A.J. Thakor. 1992. "Is Fairly Priced Deposit Insurance Possible?" *Journal of Finance* 47: 227–245.

Cooke, T. 1923. "The Collapse of Bank-Deposit Guaranty in Oklahoma and Its Position in Other States," *Quarterly Journal of Economics* 38: 109–139.

Crow, J.W. 1993. "Monetary Policy, and the Responsibilities and Accountability of Central Banks," *Bank of Canada Review* (Spring), pp. 21–30.

Diamond, D., and P. Dybvig. 1983. "Bank Runs, Deposit Insurance, and Liquidity," *Journal of Political Economy* 91: 401–419.

Easterbrook, F.H. 1983. "Anti-Trust and the Economics of Federalism," *Journal of Law and Economics* 26: 23–50.

Economic Council of Canada. 1976. *Efficiency and Regulation: A Study of Deposit Institutions*. Ottawa: Economic Council of Canada.

Estey, W.Z. 1986. *Report of the Inquiry into the Collapse of the CCB and Northland Bank*. Ottawa: Supply and Services Canada.

Evans, J.L. 1992. "Financial Services in the 90s: The Trust Perspective." Speech delivered at the 1992 Trust Companies Administrators Conference, Fredericton, New Brunswick.

Falconbridge, J.D. 1913. *The Canadian Law of Banks and Banking*. Toronto: Canada Law Book.

Friedman, M., and A. Schwartz. 1963. *A Monetary History of the United States, 1867–1960*. Princeton, NJ: Princeton University Press.

Giovannini, A. 1993. "Central Banking in a Monetary Union: Reflections on the Proposed Statute of the European Central Bank," *Carnegie-Rochester Conference Series on Public Policy* 38: 191–230.

Gisbourne, F.H., and A.A. Fraser, eds. 1922. *Reports of the Minister of Justice and Orders in Council upon the Subject of Provincial Legislation, 1896–1920*, vol. 2. Ottawa: King's Printer.

Gorbet, F.W. 1993. "Deposit Insurance Reform: A View from the Outside." North American Life Insurance Co. Toronto. Mimeographed.

Handfield-Jones, S. 1990. "Safeguarding Depositors and Investors: The Role of Deposit Insurance and Enhanced Supervision," Conference Board of Canada Report 56-90-DF. Ottawa.

Horstmann, I.J., and J.R. Markusen. 1986. "Up the Average Cost Curve: Inefficient Entry and the New Protectionism," *Journal of International Economics* 20: 225–248.

Jacklin, C., and S. Bhattacharya. 1988. "Distinguishing Panics and Information-Based Bank Runs," *Journal of Political Economy* 96: 569–592.

Kaufman, G.G. 1989. "Are Some Banks Too Large to Fail? Myth and Reality," Working Paper 89-14. Chicago: Federal Reserve Bank of Chicago.

Keeley, M. 1990. "Deposit Insurance, Risk, and Market Power," *American Economic Review* 80: 1183–1200.

Kryzanowski, L., and G.S. Roberts. 1993. "Canadian Banking Solvency, 1922–40," *Journal of Money Credit and Banking* 25: 361–376.

Laidler, D.E.W. 1991. *How Shall We Govern the Governor? A Critique of the Governance of the Bank of Canada*, The Canada Round 1. Toronto: C.D. Howe Institute.

Laskin, B. 1986. *Laskin's Canadian Constitutional Law*, 5th ed. Toronto: Carswell.

McDonald, P.N. 1972. "The B.N.A. Act and the Near Banks: A Case Study in Federalism," *Alberta Law Review* 10: 155–217.

Macey, J.R., and G.P. Miller. 1988. "Bank Failures, Risk Monitoring, and the Market for Bank Control," *Columbia Law Review* 88: 1153–1226.

————, and J.R. Miller. 1992. "Double Liability of Bank Shareholders: History and Implications," *Wake Forest Law Review* 27: 31–62.

McKeown, H.A. 1924. *Report of the Royal Commission to Inquire Into and Report Upon the Affairs of the Home Bank of Canada.* Ottawa: King's Printer.

McLeod, H.C. 1909. *Bank Inspection: The Necessity for External Examination.* Toronto.

Macmillan, L. 1933. *Report of the Royal Commission on Banking and Currency in Canada.* Ottawa: King's Printer.

Meredith, W.R. 1913. *Report of the Royal Commission on the Farmers Bank of Canada,* Sessional Paper 153a. Ottawa.

Merton, R.C., and Z. Bodie. 1993. "Deposit Insurance Reform: A Functional Approach," *Carnegie-Rochester Conference Series on Public Policy* 38: 1–34.

Miller, G.P. 1993. "Politics of Deposit Insurance Reform: The Case of Argentina." Federal Reserve Bank of Chicago, Conference on Bank Structure and Competition. Forthcoming.

Mishkin, F.S. 1992. "An Evaluation of the Treasury Plan for Banking Reform," *Journal of Economic Perspectives* 6: 133–153.

Nathan, A., and E. Neave. 1989. "Competition and Contestability in Canada's Financial System: Empirical Results," *Canadian Journal of Economics* 22: 576–594.

Neufeld, E.P. 1972. *The Financial System of Canada: Its Growth and Development.* Toronto: Macmillan.

Ontario. 1967. Legislature. *Debates.*

Parizeau, J. 1969. *Report of the Study Committee on Financial Institutions.* Quebec: Government of Quebec.

Pesando, J.E. 1986. "The Wyman Report: An Economist's Perspective," *Canadian Business Law Journal* 11: 105–120.

Porter Commission. *See* Canada. 1964.

Posner, R.A. 1992. *Economic Analysis of Law,* 4th ed. Boston: Little, Brown.

Postelwaite, A., and X. Vives. 1987. "Banks Runs as an Equilibrium Phenomenon," *Journal of Political Economy* 95: 485–491.

Reuber, G. 1993. "CDIC: Silver Anniversary Questions." Speech to the 41st Annual Meeting of the Trust Companies Association of Canada, Ottawa.

Romer, T., and B.R. Weingast. 1990. "Political Foundations of the Thrift Debacle," Working Paper E 90 22. Stanford, Cal.: Hoover Institution.

Schwartz, L.P. 1993. "Improving Federal Deposit Insurance," Discussion Paper 93-01. Queen's University. School of Policy Studies. Government and Competitiveness Project. Kingston, Ont.

Shearer, R.A., J.F. Chant, and D.E. Bond. 1984. *The Economics of the Canadian Financial System*, 2d ed. Scarborough, Ont.: Prentice-Hall of Canada.

Smith, A. [1776] 1976. *An Inquiry into the Nature and Causes of the Wealth of Nations*, edited by E. Cannon. Chicago: University of Chicago Press.

Smith, B., and R.W. White. 1988. "The Deposit Insurance System in Canada," *Canadian Public Policy* 14: 333–346.

Stigler, G.J. 1971. "A Theory of Economic Regulation," *Bell Journal of Economics and Management Science* 2: 3–21.

———. 1974. "Free Riders and Collective Action: An Appendix to Theories of Economic Regulation," *Bell Journal of Economics and Management Science* 5: 359–365.

Sutton, B., and M. Andrews. 1993. "Compensation Plans in the Canadian Financial Sector: A Comparison." Report prepared for the Department of Finance Deposit Insurance Review by the Conference Board of Canada. Ottawa.

Swinburne, M., and M. Castello-Branco. 1991. "Central Bank Independence: Issues and Experience," Working Paper 91/58. Washington, DC. International Monetary Fund.

United States. 1991. General Accounting Office. *Deposit Insurance: An Overview of Six Foreign Systems*. Report to the Chairman, Committee on Banking, Housing, and Urban Affairs. Washington, DC.

White, E.N. 1983. *The Regulation and Reform of the American Banking System, 1900–1929*. Princeton, NJ: Princeton University Press.

Wyman, R. 1985. *Final Report of the Working Committee on the Canada Deposit Insurance Corporation*. Ottawa: Queen's Printer.

Zelmer, M. 1991. "Recent Developments in the Trust and Mortgage Loan Industry," *Bank of Canada Review* (June), pp. 3–19.

Members of the
C.D. Howe Institute[*]

Air Canada
Alberta Energy Company Ltd.
Alberta Natural Gas Company Ltd.
The Alberta Stock Exchange
Alcan Aluminium Limited
American Barrick Resources Corporation
The ARA Consulting Group Inc.
ATCO Ltd.
BC Gas Inc.
BC Sugar Refinery, Limited
BC TEL
BCE Inc.
Bank of Montreal
The Bank of Nova Scotia
Banque Laurentienne du Canada
Banque Nationale du Canada
Barclays Bank of Canada
Bell Canada
Susan Bellan
Roy F. Bennett
Beutel, Goodman Company Ltd.
R.W. Billingsley
The Birks Family Foundation
The Bolt Supply House Ltd.
Bombardier Inc.
R.A.N. Bonnycastle
Gerald K. Bouey
Brascan Limited
Peter F. Bronfman
M. David R. Brown
Michael Brown
Pierre Brunet
Burns Fry Limited
Business Council of British Columbia
CAE Inc.

The CRB Foundation
The CSL Group Inc.
The Calgary Chamber of Commerce
Camdev Corporation
Canada Colors and Chemicals Limited
Canada Deposit Insurance Corporation
The Canada Life Assurance Company
Canada Overseas Investments Limited
Canada Post Corporation
Canada Trust
Canadian Association of Petroleum
    Producers
Canadian Bankers' Association
Canadian Chamber of Commerce
Canadian Corporate Funding Ltd.
Canadian Federation of Independent
    Business
Canadian Hunter Exploration Ltd.
Canadian Imperial Bank of Commerce
Canadian Labour Market and
    Productivity Centre
Canadian National
Canadian Pacific Limited
Canadian Pacific Forest Products Limited
Canadian Pulp & Paper Association
Canadian Reassurance Company
Canadian Utilities Limited
Canadian Western Bank
Chauvco Resources Ltd.
Chevron Canada Resources
Ciba-Geigy Canada Ltd.
Clairvest Group Inc.
Cogeco inc.
Communications, Energy and Paper
    Workers Union of Canada
Consumers Gas

---

[*] The views expressed in this publication are those of the authors and do not necessarily reflect the opinions of the Institute's members.

Coopers & Lybrand
E. Kendall Cork
William J. Cosgrove
Co-Steel Inc.
Pierre Côté
Cott Corporation
J.G. Crean
Crestbrook Forest Industries Ltd.
John Crispo
Crown Life Insurance Company Limited
Thomas P. d'Aquino
W. Ross DeGeer
Deloitte & Touche
Desjardins Ducharme Stein Monast
Robert Després
John H. Dickey
Iain St. C. Dobson
The Dominion of Canada General
    Insurance Company
Du Pont Canada Inc.
Marcel Dutil
Gordon H. Eberts
The Empire Life Insurance Company
H.E. English
ENSIS Corporation
Ernst & Young
Export Development Corporation
Ronald J. Farano, Q.C.
Field & Field Perraton Masuch
First Marathon Securities Limited
Aaron M. Fish
John P. Fisher
Fishery Products International Limited
C.J. Michael Flavell, Q.C.
Fleck Manufacturing Inc.
Ford Motor Company of Canada, Limited
Formula Growth Limited
L. Yves Fortier, C.C., Q.C.
Four Seasons Hotels Limited
GSW Inc.
Hilary Geller
General Electric Canada Inc.
General Motors of Canada Limited
Gluskin Sheff + Associates Inc.
Goodman & Goodman
Peter Goring
The Great-West Life Assurance Company

Greyhound Lines of Canada
Morton Gross
Le Groupe Secor Inc.
Groupe Sobeco Inc.
H. Anthony Hampson
C.M. Harding Foundation
Hawker Siddeley Canada Inc.
Lawrence L. Herman
Hewlett-Packard (Canada) Ltd.
Hill & Knowlton Canada
Hollinger Inc.
Home Oil Company Limited
Gordon J. Homer
Honeywell Limited
Hongkong Bank of Canada
The Horsham Corporation
Dezsö Horváth
Human Resources Association of
    Nova Scotia
H. Douglas Hunter
Hydro-Québec
IBM Canada Ltd.
Imasco Limited
Imperial Oil Limited
Inco Limited
Inland Cement Limited
The Insurance Bureau of Canada
Interprovincial Pipe Line Inc.
Investors Group Inc.
IPSCO Inc.
Tsutomu Iwasaki
The Jarislowsky Foundation
Robert Johnstone
KPMG Peat Marwick Thorne
Joseph Kruger II
Lac Minerals Ltd.
R.William Lawson
Jacques A. Lefebvre
Gérard Limoges
London Life Insurance Company
J.W. (Wes) MacAleer
McCallum Hill Companies
MacDonald, Dettwiler & Associates Ltd.
McKinsey & Company
Maclab Enterprises
James Maclaren Industries Inc.
Maclean Hunter Limited

Jack M. MacLeod
McMillan Binch
MacMillan Bloedel Limited
William Mackness
Mannville Oil & Gas Ltd.
The Manufacturers Life Insurance
  Company
Maple Leaf Foods Inc.
Maritime Telegraph & Telephone
  Company, Limited
Marsh & McLennan Limited
James Mauldin
The Mercantile and General
  Reinsurance Group
William M. Mercer Limited
Merck Frosst Canada Inc.
Ronald H. Meredith-Jones
Methanex Corporation
Micmac Maliseet Development
  Corporation Inc.
Miles Canada Inc.
Robert Mitchell Inc.
The Molson Companies Limited
Monsanto Canada Inc.
Montreal Trust
Moore Corporation Limited
The Mutual Life Assurance Company of
  Canada
NCR Canada Ltd.
National Trust
National Westminster Bank of Canada
Nesbitt Thomson Deacon
Noma Industries Limited
Noranda Forest Inc.
Noranda Inc.
North American Life Assurance Company
Northwood Pulp and Timber Limited
NOVA Corporation of Alberta
Ontario Hydro
The Oshawa Group Limited
James S. Palmer
PanCanadian Petroleum Limited
Pembina Corporation
Petro-Canada
Les Placements T.A.L. Ltée.
Placer Dome Inc.
David A. Potts
Power Corporation of Canada

PowerWest Financial Ltd.
Pratt & Whitney Canada Inc.
Price Waterhouse
J. Robert S. Prichard
Procor Limited
ProGas Limited
QUNO Corporation
RBC Dominion Securities Inc.
Redpath Industries Limited
Henri Remmer
Retail Council of Canada
Richardson Greenshields
  of Canada Limited
R.T. Riley
Robin Hood Multifoods Inc.
Rogers Communications Inc.
Rothschild Canada Limited
Royal Bank of Canada
ROYCO Hotels & Resorts
St. Lawrence Cement Inc.
Samuel, Son & Co., Limited
Sandwell Inc.
Sanpalo Investments Corporation
Saskoil
Guylaine Saucier
André Saumier
Sceptre Investment Counsel
Sceptre Resources Limited
Dick Schmeelk
ScotiaMcLeod Inc.
Sharwood and Company
Shell Canada Limited
Sherritt Inc.
Sidbec-Dosco Inc.
Southam Inc.
Spar Aerospace Limited
Speedy Muffler King Inc.
Speirs Consultants Inc.
Philip Spencer, Q.C.
The Standard Life Assurance Company
Strategico Inc.
Sun Life Assurance Company of Canada
Suncor Inc.
Swiss Bank Corporation (Canada)
TELUS Corporation
Laurent Thibault
3M Canada Inc.

The Toronto Dominion Bank
Toronto Star Newspaper Limited
The Toronto Stock Exchange
TransAlta Utilities Corporation
TransCanada PipeLines Limited
Trimac Limited
Trizec Corporation Ltd.
Robert J. Turner
Unilever Canada Limited
Urgel Bourgie Limitée
Manon Vennat

VIA Rail Canada Inc.
J.H. Warren
West Fraser Timber Co. Ltd.
Westcoast Energy Inc.
George Weston Limited
Alfred G. Wirth
M.K. Wong & Associates Ltd.
Wood Gundy Inc.
Fred R. Wright
Xerox Canada Inc.
Paul H. Ziff

Honorary Members

G. Arnold Hart
David Kirk
Paul H. Leman

A.M. Runciman
J. Ross Tolmie, Q.C.

About the authors.

Jack Carr and Frank Mathewson are Professors of Economics at the University of Toronto. Jack Carr has published research on monetary economics, financial markets, and economic issues in law. Frank Mathewson does research in the fields of industrial organization, competition policy, and law. Neil Quigley is Assistant Professor of Economics at the University of Western Ontario. His primary research interest is in the history of banking and financial markets. All three authors are Research Associates of the Institute for Policy Analysis at the University of Toronto.

Due